## Praise for *Healing from Hidden Abuse*

"Compassionate and well-researched, a must read for anyone healing from psychological abuse. The warm, conversational writing style and the author's professional experience combine to make the perfect recovery resource."

—**Jackson MacKenzie**, author of *Psychopath Free* and co-founder of PsychopathFree.com, an online support community that reaches millions of abuse survivors each month.

"Shannon Thomas has written an important book about something ugly, hidden, and difficult to describe. Psychological abuse. How is it possible that one person can gain so much power to destroy another person's sense of worth, safety, and sanity? Shannon tells you how, but more importantly, she gives you a roadmap that helps you wake up, break free, heal, and rebuild your shattered life."

—**Leslie Vernick LCSW**, counselor, coach, speaker, and author of *The Emotionally Destructive Marriage* and *The Emotionally Destructive Relationship*.

"Few writers are able to connect research, experience, and intuitive understanding as Shannon Thomas does in her groundbreaking new book for survivors of emotional and psychological trauma. In *Healing from Hidden Abuse*, you will find not only evidence of Shannon's expertise as a therapist who has worked with clients suffering from the trauma of covert psychological abuse, but also her powerful mastery of the crucial questions that are needed in order to work through the trauma and heal...I highly recommend this life-saving book for survivors."

—**Shahida Arabi**, author of *Becoming the Narcissist's Nightmare: How to Devalue and Discard the Narcissist While Supplying Yourself* and founder of Self-Care Haven.

"In her book, *Healing from Hidden Abuse*, Shannon Thomas offers words of wisdom and hope as she shines a spotlight on this necessary topic. Clearly she gets it, and her explanations of the steps involved in healing are spot on. Not only will you find the body of the book helpful, she goes a step further by offering a detailed guided journal at the end. This resource is a valuable tool for both therapist and patient."

—**Dr. Les Carter,** author of *Enough About You, Let's Talk About Me* and creator of MarriagePath.com.

# Healing from Hidden Abuse

## Also by Shannon Thomas

*Masterminding Our Way: The Power of 5 Minds*
(Co-authored with Sarah Gilliland, Wendy Knutson,
Lauren Midgley, and Nicole Smith)

Five professional women share their experience within a Mastermind entrepreneur group. They tell how their group started, their individual stories, and how the Mastermind group has been a benefit to their personal and business lives. Within the book, the authors provide valuable information by showing the reader how to start their own Mastermind group.

# Healing from Hidden Abuse

A Journey Through the Stages of Recovery
from Psychological Abuse

Shannon Thomas, LCSW

**MAST**
Publishing House

Healing from Hidden Abuse

© 2016 Copyright by Shannon Thomas

Published by MAST Publishing House

www.mastpublishinghouse.com

Editing by: Cassi Choi

ISBN: 978-0-9978290-8-2

DISCLAIMER

*Dedicated to
Hotstuff Thomas and Baby-face Thomas,
two joys in my life*

# CONTENTS

# ACKNOWLEDGMENTS

My clients, you are closer to my heart and dearer to me than you will ever know. I look forward to seeing you each day. We often laugh loudly together, and other times we sit in the tender moments of silence when the pain is too intense. You have taught me so much, and truly, you have made my life better than it would have been otherwise. Thank you for making a place for me in your life story.

Authors who have helped me in my own journey of healing and inspired me in my career as a therapist: Dr. Susan Forward, Leslie Vernick, and Dr. Les Carter.

Jackson Mackenzie for writing *Psychopath Free.* It stirred me to learn more about psychological abuse and the impact on survivors. You answered a question that I did not even know I needed an answer to. Thank you for not only your continued words of encouragement, but also actions of support to improve this book. I am so grateful to you, Kim Luis, and the entire Psychopath Free team. You all have my highest respect. You are gems who have taken pain and turned it into true beauty.

All the advocates within the psychological abuse recovery community who share my work with your followers. Your support is a daily source of encouragement. Thank you for your dedication to the blogs and social media pages you manage. Only other advocates know how much time and care goes into maintaining a healthy online community. Thank you for creating and sustaining a place of healing for survivors. Lilly Hope Lucario, you are a shining example of what an empowered survivor can accomplish. Your advocacy work to educate others is admirable. A special thank you to Shahida Arabi for your support and collaboration in reaching people with the message of healing and hope.

Dr. Aesha John, Dr. D. Lynn Jackson, Texas Christian University (TCU) Institutional Review Board, and the entire TCU Department of Social Work for your encouragement of the 2016 research project: *Examining Patterns of Psychological Abuse.*

Cassi Choi for being a wonderful friend and editor. I am truly grateful for your dedication. Also, the long hours to unravel my thoughts and helping them make sense on the pages. I appreciate your patience as I struggled to understand grammar rules and your willingness to support me as I willfully break some of them.

My entrepreneur role models, think tank members, and quasi-Board of Directors: Lauren Midgley, Wendy Knutson, and Nicole Smith. When I reflect on the individuals who have helped me develop and grow as a business owner and woman, you three incredible ladies are at the top of the list. There is no way this project would have been completed without each of your wisdom and direct input. You challenge me in ways that are uncomfortable at times, and that is exactly the type of business associates every entrepreneur must have in her life.

My bestie and doppleganger, Rhonda Lindley. Having you in my life has healed a place deep within my soul that needed restoration. You have helped me feel less orphaned in the world. Your beautiful spirit, witty humor, and sassiness are refreshing waters in parched places.

My funny and gentle rock of a husband, Hotstuff. Your humor and joy make me smile every day. Of anyone, you know the depth of my own recovery journey, the messiness of being married to a survivor of childhood trauma, and also the wholeness that can come through healing. There simply are no words to express my gratitude for your endless patience, encouragement, and for never trying to clip my wings. You have watched me flourish into almost a completely different person during our marriage. You are an example of a man who wants his wife to grow, morph, and change for the better; without being threatened by her new found inner strength and independent spirit. I am forever grateful that we have chosen one another to climb the mountain together.

My beloved son, Baby-face. I know you're not an actual baby, but you will always be my baby. You are my inspiration. Your inner strength and maturity beyond your years are attributes that I so deeply admire about you. Thank you for your wise words of encouragement to me. They have been just the boost I needed during this writing project. You, precious baby, have a story inside of you to share with the world. I cannot wait to be a part of making that happen one day. Your life story needs to be told in order for others to see that love does heal.

# INTRODUCTION

Within every community, toxic people can be found hiding in families, couples, companies, and places of worship. The insidious and cryptic nature of psychological abuse leaves a wake of individuals left to pick up the pieces of their shattered emotions, self-esteem, and aspects of life functioning. You may be able to identify with feeling overwhelmed by the hidden actions of someone in your life. If so, then you are in the right place. People who have experienced psychological abuse often cannot clearly describe what has been done to them. You may find yourself in the situation of trying to sort out a romantic relationship that has kept you feeling like you are a yo-yo. Come close, go away. Repeat. It could be your family, or in-laws, who have made you their token scapegoat and family punching bag. You may be experiencing grief symptoms. You could be mourning the loss of the relationship you thought you would be receiving. Abusers can also be bosses or co-workers who appear to take pleasure in making your daily life miserable. Perhaps the harm you have experienced is within a place of worship. You let your guard completely down only to find yourself repeatedly stabbed in the back. Perhaps made to feel guilty for standing up for yourself.

People who have experienced hidden abuse know things are not normal. You feel it and sometimes you can even see solid glimpses of the dysfunction. More often than not though, it is like a snake. It moves quickly and slithers away before you can get a good look at it. You may have tried to explain to people the exact harm that has been done to you. I bet it often comes out sounding as if you are exceptionally needy, petty, or even paranoid. Without a specific set of terms to describe the actions of a hidden abuser, targets of this type of harm feel frustrated with their inability to make other people see the games that are being played. This happens because the average person doesn't know about psychological abuse. Unless you have the precise education needed to be able to explain the situation, the toxic person's plan works. They want to remain secretive about the abuse. They purposefully hide their behaviors just under the public radar. When people try to complain about them, the complaints fall flat on the floor. The abuser walks away looking "squeaky clean," and the victim appears unstable. I am sure you would agree it is infuriating. Psychological abuse is perhaps one of the most hidden injustices of our times because it leaves the targets unable to trust even themselves. It is as if their lives are being violently shaken, like one would shake a snow globe, and everything is swirling in chaos.

Why is psychological abuse also referred to as hidden abuse? The behaviors of the abuser(s) involve chronic and repetitive secret games being played by one individual, or a group of people against a target. These actions are so well disguised that their venom frequently goes unnoticed. It is similar to clear toxins placed in a glass of water; one cannot see the injury being done until the body starts reacting to the prolonged exposure of the poison. This is exactly the way abusers plan it with psychological abuse. Covert, hidden, sneaky, and off the radar are all part of their agenda. As their relationships progress, so does the game playing. Eventually their actions might become more overt and then, sometimes, noticeable. By the time these outward signs of dysfunction reveal themselves, the targets of the abuse are usually very devastated. They have been successfully manipulated to wonder if they are the problem, perhaps even the actual toxic person in the relationship.

When people begin counseling, many decide to come in so they can fix themselves. They are convinced if only they could become stronger they wouldn't be treated so poorly. Most people who are willing to invest in counseling are capable of being self-reflective. They are able to do the hard work and deal with their own negative behaviors. Psychological abusers are banking on the other person changing because the abusers never will. Later in our time together, I will explain why this is true. For now, I want you to know that all people who have encountered a hidden abuser blame themselves at some point. The reason individuals take on the blame is because they believe they wouldn't be treated so badly by family, loved ones, colleagues, or in their place of worship if something wasn't really wrong with them. In the environment of psychological abuse, the depths of self-hatred a target experiences can be overwhelming. Figuring out the truth is part of the process to unravel the massive amount of lies that have been spun by the abuser.

As a therapist, I have had the privilege of walking with many people through the healing process. It is an incredible honor to be welcomed into people's lives. While you and I journey through this material, I will be sharing themes, commonly known concepts within the recovery community, and information from a research project that I completed as co-investigator. Out of my deep respect for the individuals who have entrusted me with the intimate details of their lives, I will not be sharing snippets of real people's stories. Even with identifying information taken out, it is not right to use their experiences as examples. What I will do is highlight fictional stories to show the patterns that are present within psychological abuse. Seeing the connections between what you may be experiencing and what other people have walked through is very helpful to find your own

*You are not alone in having witnessed some of the most bizarre human behaviors. It's important for you to know that truth.*

healing. You are not alone in having witnessed some of the most bizarre human behaviors. It's important for you to know that truth.

Many people wonder how psychological abuse and emotional abuse differ. Are they perhaps the same thing? For me, they are two distinctly different forms of abuse. I believe that people can be emotionally abusive but still have empathy for others. Example? Loved ones who are struggling with addiction will harm others while living out their cravings. Their core personhood includes care for others, but it is masked through the haze of a drug or alcohol controlled life. They harm others while in their own lethal state. Once the addiction is fully addressed through recovery, most of these individuals are able to make an authentic amends for the harm they caused. On the other side of the coin, psychological abusers damage others—not out of impaired judgment—but because they enjoy the control they gain from abusing people. Shocking, right? It's often hard to even comprehend such human ugliness exists in the world. I assure you it does. You most likely already know it. Psychological abusers play games with their targets and know precisely what they are doing. Some will even admit they enjoy being the puppet master and keeping people off balance for their own entertainment. Others don't outwardly disclose it, but their enjoyment comes bleeding through with a casual smirk or hateful chuckle.

If you have picked up this book, I can probably assume a couple of things about you. The cover of the book or title caught your eye, or you're interested in knowing more about the recovery process from psychological abuse. Maybe all three. Perhaps there are other reasons that the idea of recovering from hidden abuse is needed. The truth is that toxic people are everywhere. Too many individuals have had their lives rocked by an abuser. There are few resources to turn to for therapeutic support when sorting through the pain left behind specifically by psychological abuse. Most people have no clue hidden abuse is taking place right under their noses. It is being perpetrated by individuals who would never be suspected of being abusers. The concealed nature of this harm is what leaves its targets devastated. Some hide their pain better than others, but all targets of abuse suffer in some deep personal way.

*Most people have no clue hidden abuse is taking place right under their noses. It is being perpetrated by individuals who would never be suspected of being abusers. The concealed nature of this harm is what leaves its targets devastated.*

The majority of people who have been abused psychologically do not believe they will ever make it through the first stage of recovery (*Despair*). The early period of recovery is lonely. It is the emotional equivalent of having dry, weary bones. People describe this time as having been completely sucked dry of joy and energy. Can you relate to those descriptions? The days of feeling sparkly and clear-headed have long been gone, or maybe never existed because of childhood abuse. Good feelings have been replaced with anxiety, and perhaps a constant sense of gloom. Doesn't sound fun, right? It's not. I do hope that if you find yourself in a state of despair, you will keep reading. There is life after psychological abuse. I know it may not seem like that today. If I could ask you to trust me, I would. I know that if your life path has crossed with an abuser, trust has long left your emotional tool box. I completely understand. Nonetheless, hang in there. Let's see how you feel by the end of the recovery stages.

As I sat down to write this book, I knew there were a million things I could talk about on the topic. I am aware that when someone is seeking information on healing from hidden abuse, it is important to get to the nuggets of truth as soon as possible. If you picked up this book because you are wondering what in the world has happened to you regarding a relationship in your life, then I want to say: welcome, friend. Now is a perfect time to take a deep breath, relax your muscles as much as you can, and if the tears come, that's okay. Tears don't freak us out around here. Men cry, women cry. It's all good. If you're like me and not really a crier, that's okay too. This is a space and a place to be real. If you have found yourself in the vortex of an emotional storm, finding a quiet spot to heal is vitally important. I hope this book will be helpful to you in some way on your journey of recovery.

Perhaps you may feel that you have played some

role in the dysfunction. We will take an honest look at that later on in the six stages of recovery. You might say relationships are 50/50 in responsibility. This is not necessarily true, and most definitely not when one person is clinically toxic. There will be aspects of the role you played in the relationship that we will need to look at and address. As a therapist, almost every client has heard me say, "Watch your toes, I am about to step on them." This is because counseling isn't just commiserating about the vulgar person and everything he or she did that was utterly unacceptable. Of course, we do spend time shaking our heads at the sheer arrogance by which psychologically abusive people govern their lives. At some point, we have to get to the work of moving on to healing. Talking about the messy stuff does happen in recovery. Toes getting stepped on is part of the journey. However, all therapeutic work must be done with gentleness and with the utmost respect. That is my promise to you within the pages of this book.

No one book, workbook, blog post, or meme will pull all the pieces together for each and every person. Collectively, they can work together to help make sense of the turmoil that comes from having been or being in contact with toxic people. My intent is to show you the process people go through when they come to therapy with me as a counselor. It does not imply a therapeutic relationship with each reader. If you feel working with a counselor could be helpful, I encourage you to do so in your local area. You can also find a life coach who specializes in this type of mistreatment. I know finding someone who understands psychological abuse can be tricky. That is why I have provided some trusted resources in the back of the book.

In my private practice, I specialize in working with survivors of psychological abuse. Having done this work for many years, I have identified what I believe are the six stages all survivors go through when healing from toxic encounters. Your abuse may have taken place in your family of origin, in a romantic relationship, within a friend group, at work, or at a place of worship like a church or ministry. The six stages of recovery from hidden abuse are applicable no matter the location of the abuse.

*The six stages of recovery from hidden abuse are applicable no matter the location of the abuse.*

I find it interesting that the healing process for this form of abuse is remarkably similar, regardless of the setting. This is because psychological abusers share common character traits. Many of us in the abuse recovery community sadly joke that there seems to be some sick psychological abuse manual out there being passed around. We say this because many of the exact same abusive behaviors are across race, age, gender, sexual orientation, geography, and language. *Stage Two: Education,* is specifically designed to help you decipher the abusive behaviors that are most commonly seen in hidden psychological abuse.

It is extremely powerful when someone new to recovery realizes they are not "crazy." This form of harm is like an ever-changing maze. Once people start to see the patterns, the abusers abruptly shift tactics. The victims are again lost in their search for the truth. Once you have the necessary education, your confidence will increase. That is a good thing because we are unable to heal from what we cannot, or will not, acknowledge exists.

Another assumption I can make while writing this book is some people reading it will have been on their journey of recovery for years. Some folks will be in the middle of their process; having some knowledge but needing more. Then there will be women and men who are right in the thick of being metaphorically tossed in a raging ocean and can't find the surface. In their confusion, a lot of people may be swimming to the bottom of the ocean floor rather than coming up for air. That can be a very scary place to be in life. Hang tight. I hope that working through the six stages of recovery will help you find the fresh air needed for sustaining life.

Recognizing you've been a part of an abusive relationship is a process. Psychological abuse doesn't leave bruises. There are no broken bones. There are no holes in the walls. The bruises, brokenness, and holes are held tightly within the survivor. The abuser wants it exactly that way. Keeping their hands clean and being able to project a public persona are hallmarks of psychological abusers. Coming to a full understanding of exactly how abusers operate helps survivors find their breath again.

Education will make the spinning of confusion stop. That probably sounds pretty good to you. This knowledge can help you recognize future toxic people, and the red flags they wave. Some flags are very small. Once you have gone through the healing experience, you will spot them. Don't worry. You're not likely to be sideswiped again by a covert (hidden) or overt (aggressive) abuser. No one wants to go from a relationship with one of these individuals to yet another. That cycle must stop, and it can in recovery.

A day does not go by that I don't hear a person openly question how they ended up in a relational mess. One of the big aha moments comes when people realize that they were specifically targeted. Yes, you were spotted and chosen. There are many reasons why this is true, and we will go into greater detail later on. Psychological abusers set out to trick people, and they know exactly what they do. They actually know better than anyone the lies they tell, the games they play, and the enjoyment they derive from controlling others. You may not agree with me and wonder if they are just victims of their own life circumstances. As we walk along together, I hope to change your mind about their lack of knowledge. Yes, I want to change this viewpoint you might hold. I desire to do so because I strongly believe that until victims know deep in their souls that it is a choice to be an abuser, they will continue to entertain pity for toxic people. That mental trap has no place in recovery. We cannot feel badly for those who intentionally harm us.

If we do, we will not be free from their heavy chains. Pity gives way to excuses and excuses will soften the heart of anyone. It's a part of the human condition. It is the double-edged sword of compassion. Those who have been targeted are often very empathetic people. They may identify with being sensitive spirited. In the recovery community, it is called being an Empath. The dance between an empath and an abuser is one of control, mind games, and mockery. This is why education is such a critical step in the healing process. Tenderness from empaths will be used against them time and time again by psychological abusers.

In *Healing from Hidden Abuse*, we have a lot of material to cover. My desire is that you will not feel rushed to quickly get through it from cover to cover. I enjoy reading books slowly, and reflecting on the words I have read. I will often sit down with a pen in hand and underline key phrases or sentences that jump out at me. That way, I can later go back and quickly remind myself of the nuggets that originally were meaningful. I would encourage you to do the same here. If you do push through this material, maybe consider coming back around for a second read and taking time to reflect a little more slowly. There is also a Personal Reflections journal at the back of this book that can help you personalize the experience. The journal questions are designed to be used on your own or in a small group setting.

It is up to you to decide how best to absorb this material. I really hope you can interact with the concepts. What do I mean? Write down ideas that pop into your head as you read. Disagree with me when you come across something that doesn't work for you. Give a loud shout of "Oh yes!" when you read something that completely resonates. I am from Texas so you could also throw in an "Oh yes, y'all!" should you feel so inclined, but no pressure to southernize yourself. Basically, take an active role in reading. Do not simply absorb the words passively. As someone who has encountered a psychological abuser, your passivity was demanded to make that relationship work. Your recovery is living in the opposite spirit of being emotionally brow beaten into looking down at the ground. Your healing is about standing up tall, looking people in the eyes, and calmly saying, "I have my own opinions, and I am okay if you disagree." Go ahead and read this book in that powerful stance. I want you to find your inner strength. A strong individual makes for a challenge to the abuser. Guess what? That's my exact goal. I want anyone who reads this book to become a royal pain to any would-be future abuser.

As I said before, my desire is to highlight as best I can the process that clients go through when they walk into my office. I am going to take us step-by-step of how I work with a new client. As a therapist who specializes in recovery from hidden psychological abuse, I have journeyed with men and women through the therapeutic process that must take place for people to heal and move forward. You might not even know if you have been a part of a toxic relationship. I want this book to serve as a resource for you. If after reading it you find out that you are not, or have not been, in a psychologically abusive relationship, then your time has not been wasted. You will now know very clearly what one does look like. This knowledge can help you going forward. You may be called upon to share the information with a loved one who might be trapped in a toxic connection. The more people who know the signs of psychological abuse, the better. Abusers count on never being called out for their behaviors. They think they have everyone around them fooled. They often openly gloat about it. Collective societal knowledge of this form of abuse will make a difference. The longer psychological abuse lingers in the shadows, people will continue to have their lives silently and slowly ruined.

# 2016 RESEARCH PROJECT

## Examining Patterns of Psychological Abuse

A little background as to how this book came to be: in January 2016 I had the opportunity to be the co-investigator of the research project, *Examining Patterns of Psychological Abuse.* I am continually grateful to Dr. Aesha John of Texas Christian University (TCU) who served as Principal Investigator. Also, to the leadership of the TCU Department of Social Work who lent us their support and encouragement. Interjected throughout our time together, I will share some of the findings of the research as it relates to the specific topic we are discussing. I am delighted to have completed the project and to intertwine the data into the six stages of recovery that are the foundation of this book. If research is sort of a snoozefest for you, please feel free to skip this section, and move on to the next chapter. My feelings won't be hurt. Perhaps you will come back to it later and find something interesting. On the other hand, if the data intrigues you, then let's take a look together.

The research project was an online survey and we recruited participants through social media posts. Participants were asked to anonymously answer questions related to the following demographic information:

- Age
- Gender
- Ethnicity
- How is/was the perpetrator related to you?
- When were you in this relationship?
- Do you still have contact with the abusive person?

We had 623 participants opt into the study. 38% were in the 41-50 age range, 23% were 51-60 years old, and 20% were 33-40 years old. The remaining percentages were outside of those ranges.

Ninety-six percent (96%) of the participants identified as female, 4% male, and 0% transgendered. As you can see, the majority of the participants of our study self-identified as female. I do believe far more men have experienced psychological abuse than our study reflected. I have witnessed it firsthand in my counseling practice. Historically, half of my psychological abuse recovery clients have been men. I believe further research should be conducted to help gain a larger male voice on this topic. For now, I want to say to the gentlemen out there, we know your experience is just as harmful and devastating as the female experience. Generalizing, men often do not talk about what is happening behind closed doors. Please know that those of us in the recovery community know you are out there, and we want to share your stories with dignity and respect.

In the ethnicity category, 87% selected Caucasian (non-Hispanic), 5% as Hispanic, and 3% as African American. As with gender, I know this is an inherent bias in our study, based on the recruitment methods used through my professional social media contacts. Further research studies should be done to get a broader scope of just how far reaching psychological abuse is within our culture. I know from my practice, and from what can be observed with online support groups, psychological abuse affects people across all ethnic groups and nationalities.

Regarding the time frame since the abuse: 52% of the respondents are currently in the relationship, or were within the last two years; 22% were in the relationship two-five years ago; the third largest group represented 14% and were in the relationship more than 15 years ago. This is an interesting spread depicting when people were in their relationships with abusers.

I will return to the data regarding how the participants were related to the perpetrator, and if they still have contact. Those questions need a little more explanation than I want to give at this point. We will get there though.

The narrative portion of the study asked people to give answers, in their own words, to the following questions:

- Please provide specific examples of what you do to stay emotionally safe and healthy, before, during, and/or after contact with the abusive person - (295 individual responses).

- Please provide specific examples of what was the breaking point when you went "No Contact" with the abusive person (No Contact is when a victim no longer participates in contact of any form with the perpetrator) - (296 individual responses).
- Please provide specific examples of your support system. The support system can be informal (e.g., friends, other abuse survivors) or formal (e.g., therapy) - (597 individual responses).
- "Gaslighting" is when the abusive person attempts to change the facts of conversations or events in order to discredit the victim's trust in his/her own memory. If you experienced this, please provide specific examples of when you experienced gaslighting - (548 individual responses).
- "Flying Monkey" is a term to describe the individuals who surround a perpetrator and do their "dirty work," willingly or by accident. If you have experienced this, please provide specific examples of when you experienced Flying Monkey(s) - (483 individual responses).
- "Smear Campaign" is when lies, gossip, and triangulation are used by the abusive person to turn other people, or groups of other people, against a victim. If you have experienced this, please provide specific examples of how your perpetrator used a Smear Campaign against you - (527 individual responses).
- "Love Bombing" is when a toxic person uses calculated positive attention in order to manipulate the

victim's emotions and expectations of attention in the relationship. This is usually done at the beginning of the relationship. If you experienced this, please share specific examples of how your perpetrator used Love Bombing - (497 individual responses).

- "Hoovering" is when the toxic person tries to get the victim to re-engage in the relationship by sucking the victim back into contact. The hoovering can either be positive attention from the toxic person or negative attention to engage the victim in an argument, etc. If you have experienced this, please provide specific examples of how your perpetrator used Hoovering - (504 individual responses).
- If your perpetrator used spirituality or religious beliefs as manipulation to keep you in the relationship, please share specific examples - (399 individual responses).

If you are new to recovery, some of the terms Dr. John and I used in the research project may be foreign to you. That is perfectly okay. In *Stage Two: Education*, I will cover each one of these and a few more. I will also provide fictional examples based on the numerous stories I have encountered. I wanted to share a bit of the research project with you so you can have an understanding of how this book came to be, and share with you some of the data we found by doing the study. I will not be sharing specific statements the participants made in their narratives. Rather, I will be staying with the themes that emerged. All participants were able to complete their surveys confidentially. Even with that level of privacy, their stories are their own. The collective "voice" we heard will be highlighted, and I will stick to the big picture of the patterns within psychological abuse. I have witnessed the exact same characteristics in both my private counseling practice as well as within the research project. If nothing else, psychological abusers are consistent in how they abuse.

# THE BASICS OF PSYCHOLOGICAL ABUSE

# SURVIVORS

As we get started with the recovery process, I want to highlight that going forward I will be referring to people who have been the victims of psychological abuse as "survivors." Why do I do this? It is part of the common language among advocates involved in the abuse recovery community and with good cause.

The American Heritage Dictionary definition of survivor is:

> SURVIVOR: *To remain alive; to carry on despite hardships or trauma; persevere, to remain functional or usable, to live longer than; outlive, to persist or remain usable through, and to cope with a trauma or setback, to persevere after.*

I like that description. I really like the words "to carry on," "persevere," and "to remain functional." I know you might not feel very functional right at this moment. I would argue that if you have the wherewithal to find this book, buy it, and sit down to try and read through the material, you might be functioning better than you thought. Showing up for life every day is functioning. Yes, you probably want to feel healthier than you currently do, and can remember a better time pre-abuse. Perhaps your abuse was during childhood so you've only known being emotionally harmed. Even then, survivors sense they are meant to live higher quality lives than they have experienced. They long for it somewhere deep within themselves.

I use the term survivor to describe what some might call a victim. I hope you can embrace the word survivor because it is meant as a compliment. It may seem odd to think of yourself as a survivor. You might be thinking, "What have I survived? I am barely making it each day." I would ask that if it feels uncomfortable, you overlook it for now and keep reading. In the end, you may find you can better identify with the true meaning of the word. For me, those who have been in psychologically abusive relationships are not merely victims. They are people who have learned to overcome an insidious form of abuse. They have come out on the other side of healing as stronger, and often times, more confident people. I will never go so far as to say survivors should thank their abusers or view abuse as a gift. Some people advocate for that sort of thinking, but I find it harmful. I believe it gives destructive people more fuel for their emotional rampages. Any

*Any personal growth that comes after abuse is a testimony to the strength of the survivor.*

personal growth that comes after abuse is a testimony to the strength of the survivor.

I recently saw an online meme that said, "I just wanted a soul mate. I didn't want a degree in psychology." It made me laugh because to accurately understand psychological abuse, one must recognize personality disorders. These disorders are often just skimmed over in graduate-level counseling and social work programs. I assure you there are more survivors out there who understand psychological abuse than there are therapists who really "get it." If you have been a survivor who has tried counseling—either with the abuser in the same room or without—I bet more than a few of you have had less than stellar experiences. Some counseling has also turned out to be abusive. If you are someone who knows exactly what I am talking about, please let me apologize in proxy of those therapists. Some just didn't know what they were dealing with, and others are abusers themselves. Toxic people can be found everywhere, even in the mental health field. Counseling can be a wonderful resource for survivors. Please keep looking in your local area for someone who either understands psychological abuse or is willing to be educated so they are ready for your sessions. Knowledge within the counseling world must be uniform regarding how therapists are educated on the signs of psychological abuse and treatment for survivors. I can assure you many advocates are doing what they can to spearhead the needed changes.

As we begin our walk through the stages of recovery, I want to say it is a privilege to accompany you and be a part of your healing. I absolutely love the work that I get to do. It is a joy to have clients come to my office, grab a water or soda out of the refrigerator, sit down on the couch, and get to the business of putting the pieces of their lives back together. People have shared with me their best and worst moments. I am deeply touched by their authenticity and willingness to deal with life in all its messiness. I hope you can enjoy some of the same mojo, vibe, or spirit that is present in the office. Some of what we will talk about might hit right at home with you. Other topics won't apply and that is okay. A well-known substance abuse recovery program has a saying that encourages people to take what works and leave behind what does not. I encourage you to adopt that approach to everything you read on psychological abuse, including my own efforts. Not all survivors are exactly the same, nor are abusive environments. One approach to recovery will not work for everyone. The freedom to be an individual is exactly what abusers try to steal. Finding the specific path to restoration that works for you is the only thing that matters.

I want to briefly discuss the *Who, What, Where, When, How, and Why* of toxic people. I will not be going into as much depth as these topics could warrant because I would rather spend the bulk of our time on your healing, not on the abusers. They have already taken enough from you and don't deserve extra attention in this recovery process. My goal is to give enough information so you have the context to understand what's going on with these people who choose to remain abusive; even though they have all the evidence before them to seek out help for themselves.

# WHO, WHAT, WHERE, WHEN, HOW, AND WHY

## *Who* is a Psychological Abuser?

Throughout this book, I will intermittently use the terms "toxic person" or "toxic people." When I do so, I am referring to those individuals who fit the criteria for Narcissistic Personality Disorder (aka the narcissist) and Anti- Social Personality Disorder (aka the sociopath or psychopath). Later in the *What* section, I will go into greater detail regarding narcissists, sociopaths, and psychopaths. Also, we will discuss how their personalities were developed and why they choose to stay personality disordered. This is important information for any survivor to have and understand. For now, let me just say they are void of empathy and cause considerable damage to those around them. You already knew that to be true.

Who are these people? A narcissist, sociopath, or psychopath could be your mom, dad, brother, sister, grandparent, aunt, uncle, cousin, boyfriend, girlfriend, husband, wife, adult child, friend, in-laws, co-worker, boss, pastor, mentor or any other title that exists in human relationships. As you can see, their toxicity can impact many people. Their circle of influence (and therefore destruction) is sadly widespread.

### Females Are Abusers Too

The stereotype is that only men are narcissists, sociopaths, and psychopaths. That is completely incorrect. There are many women who are the cause of intense relational harm. In fact, I have had nearly as many male clients who have been survivors of hidden abuse as I have had female clients. The manner in which the female abuser operates is somewhat different than a male abuser. It is often more covert (i.e., sneaky). This isn't always true, and some are very aggressive. One of the first things you will learn about psychological abuse is related to the spectrum of behaviors. I will say that some are this way, some are that way, and it will all be true. That is one reason spotting a psychological abuser is so tricky. They take on many shapes and personalities. The core inherent faulty thinking of abusers is that everything revolves around them. The specifics of how they have manifested that belief in their lives varies from person to person.

As I mentioned before, I was co-investigator on the research project related to psychological abuse. In the two weeks the survey was open, we had 623 individuals complete the online questions. The first 500 participants came within four days of the survey being available. I was incredibly pleased, but not entirely shocked. People who have experienced the complexity of abuse by a toxic person are hungry for answers. Once they have found them, these are exceptionally generous people who want to tell their stories in the hopes of helping others through the recovery process.

One of the questions on the survey asked how the perpetrator of abuse was related to the survivor. Of the 603 individuals who responded to this question, 121 (20%) answered that their abuser was a relative (e.g., parent, sibling, child, grandparent). Of those 121 people, 87 wrote in the type of family abuser, and 41 times "Mom" (or "Mother-in-law" or "Step-mom") was entered. The title of "Parent" was entered 27 times, and "Father" 8 times. These numbers show that among the participants of the study, "Mom" (or a mom figure) was the primary family abuser. Let me state it again, women can be psychological abusers and are out there doing as much damage as their male abuser counterparts.

### The Male Abuser

In our research findings, of the 603 participants, 433 (72%) responded that the perpetrators of their abuse were romantic interests (e.g., spouses, partners, boyfriends, or girlfriends). Of the 433 respondents, 102 answered specifically what type of relationship they have, or had, with their abusers: 31 wrote in "Boyfriend; 30 said, "Spouse;" 27 were "Husband." This data tells me many of the people who completed the survey questions are in, or have been in, a romantic relationship with a toxic male.

The abusive male fits into our cultural stereotype. Domestic violence advocates have created more awareness regarding the damage of abuse. However, within many local and state jurisdictions, domestic aggression is not considered a real threat until it involves bodily harm. This leaves adults and children literally terrorized in their own homes, and nothing can legally be done. If someone has a hard time proving physical violence, how far is a survivor going to get in trying to explain the intense mind games of twisting reality that are the cornerstone of psychological abuse? I can tell you—not far at all. Survivors who try to get help to protect themselves and their children are often seen as hysterical, crazy, and unstable. This is because the covert nature of hidden abuse is very difficult to put into words. Without the correct language, survivors often sound obsessed. Those of us in the recovery community know that is not the issue at all, but the general public still has much to learn about hidden psychological abuse. That is precisely why *Stage Two: Education* is vitally important. This chapter will give you the language needed to explain the harm with which you have lived, worked, or found somewhere else in your community.

## *What* is a Psychological Abuser?

Narcissists, sociopaths, and psychopaths walk among us. It's true. As a therapist, I can diagnosis adults as

Narcissistic Personality Disordered (NPD) or Anti-Social Personality Disordered (ASPD). We do not typically diagnose personality disorders before an individual has reached adulthood. The thinking is that personalities are still forming throughout the teenage years. Some people do show characteristics of NPD or ASPD early on in life, and those kids or teens are often given another diagnosis that is not personality related.

Most people who fit the criteria for diagnosis as a narcissist, sociopath, or psychopath are never officially diagnosed because very few ever regularly attend counseling. If they do end up sitting on a therapist's couch, it is most likely because someone forced them there, or they were coming to convince the therapist they are not the problem. As a counselor, I cannot diagnose someone who is not a client. When survivors come to see me, we can talk about the criteria for diagnosis of NPD or ASPD, but I cannot diagnose someone who has never come into the office. There are all sorts of ethical issues with even hinting at a diagnosis. However, there is considerable power in survivors knowing what they have been dealing with, and having names to put to the behaviors they have witnessed. With the goal of recovery for the survivor in mind, we discuss all the characteristics of these two diagnoses without ever formally giving a diagnosis to someone who isn't a client (aka the abuser). Gaining knowledge on personality disorders is a step that cannot be missed when a survivor begins counseling.

People often ask what the clinical differences are between a narcissist, sociopath, and psychopath. I will use these fictional examples to highlight the subtle differences:

A **Narcissist** will run you over and scold you for being in their way. They will endlessly complain about how you damaged their car.

A **Sociopath** will run you over, scold you for being in their way, and have a smirk because secretly they get entertainment out of the chaos they've created.

A **Psychopath** will go to great lengths and take calculated steps to ensure they run you over, laugh while doing it, and back up to make sure the most damage is done.

Lovely people, right? That is precisely why you are beginning the hard work of recovery. While these examples above are very simplistic, they do illustrate the spectrum that is present with Narcissistic Personality Disorder and Anti-Social Personality Disorder. The differences between the three terms of narcissist, sociopath, and psychopath centers around the intensity of toxicity that is present within the individual who chooses to remain disordered and not address their lack of authentic attachments to other people.

### *Where* do psychological abusers do their harm?

Abuse can happen from one *individual* to another (e.g., parent-child, romantic, workplace, or friendships) or within a *group* (e.g., among family members, in the workplace, within groups of people, or in religious organizations).

## Individual Abusers

### The Toxic Love Interest or Spouse

There are many different ways a romantic partner can perpetrate hidden psychological abuse. I have witnessed some of the most hateful and evil abuse occur in what was expected to be a safe relationship. I have watched clients become so poisoned by their "romantic" relationships that they required hospitalization for health issues directly related to the psychological abuse. It's beyond tragic for me to sit back—with nothing more than a willingness to help—and have to watch some people deteriorate right before my eyes.

The person who was intended to be the safe harbor in their life is actually silently drowning them. This is done right in plain sight, too. Frequently, the emotional homicide is happening while other people go on clamoring about what a great guy or gal the abuser is and how lucky the survivor is to be connected to the abuser. For those who have been harmed in a

*Frequently, the emotional homicide is happening while other people go on clamoring about what a great guy or gal the abuser is and how lucky the survivor is to be connected to the abuser.*

partner relationship, you know quite well the "Jekyll and Hyde" act these individuals have perfected. What is seen behind closed doors is radically different than the public persona she or he is selling to the world. Boy, is the world buying it, too. Some of the worst hidden abusers not only have good public images, but often it is stellar. Do not for a second think that is a coincidence. In order to discredit any claims of harm a survivor might make, the abuser uses a calculated strategy. No allegations will stick in this sort of environment. The survivor ends up looking like the "crazy one," and the abuse cycle continues to spin. People should never underestimate a psychological abuser's ability to hide the truth. They are not even honest with themselves and truly believe their own lies.

I often compare the romantic attention of a hidden abuser to someone pushing drugs. How are they alike? A dealer will give "free" samples of a highly addictive drug until the target is hooked; the target becomes physically and emotionally dependent. Then, the drug is no longer freely given, but it is supplied at a very high price. That price may even be the target's self-worth and safety. If the target begins to pull away from dependency on the drug, guess what happens? More free samples until the target is hooked again. A vicious cycle of dangling the person between addiction and a high cost occurs. Vicious indeed. The extreme highs and lows of a psychologically abusive relationship often mirror that of addictions. The lows include intense anxiety and confusion. The highs are a rush of adrenaline. Recovery begins when survivors realize that the entire experience is manufactured by the psychological abuser. This tactic is done to keep the target off balance and addicted to the high moments.

I mentioned the spectrum of behaviors before, and not all abusers are pushing the survivors to the brink of instability. Some are quietly deteriorating the person's self-esteem through the emotional game of abandonment. Being present physically but checked out emotionally is not a marriage or a relationship. There is more than one way to leave someone. The various forms of hidden abuse are included in those ways. Psychological abusers often utilize means of control that are passive-aggressive. It can be very hard to see exactly what they are doing. This is why survivors wonder if they are being too sensitive or insecure. Checking out and emotionally withdrawing are ways psychological abusers like to maintain their dominance in their relationships. It's the game of who cares less. Whoever is less invested wins, right? That's how abusers think, anyway. Their "come close, then disappear" act creates all sorts of internal discord for the survivor, and the abuser loves it. Yes, they abuse on purpose. These mental games kill any level of connection a couple may have ever experienced. The ability of the abuser to harm someone close to him or her fits perfectly into the lack of relational attachment that is present within all psychological abusers.

Even while on their honeymoon, some married

survivors have experienced a radical shift in a toxic person's behavior. Survivors have shared that immediately following the wedding (like the night of the wedding), the attitude of the narcissist, sociopath, or psychopath became callous, distant, and demanding. Prior to the wedding there may have been small red flags, but nothing to warrant calling it off. Sadly, after the survivor was fully committed (or trapped) is when the mask fell. The true nature of the toxic person was then revealed. This is incredibly devastating for a newlywed who thought they were marrying the love of their life. This is especially true after a day of publicly celebrating their bond to one another. This situation is not the norm within psychologically abusive relationships, but it happens frequently enough that it warrants being mentioned.

Another situation that can arise within a toxic marriage occurs when children begin to come into the family. Survivors have shared that their spouse may have shown early red flags of being an abuser, but their negative behaviors greatly increased after the addition of children. Why does this happen? Psychological abusers are known for becoming jealous of any attention not being given to them. This jealously can occur even with their own children and spouse. Toxic people demand constant attention to sat-

> *Psychological abusers are known for becoming jealous of any attention not being given to them.*

isfy their high sense of entitlement and inflated ego. As children are born, obviously the focus cannot always be on the abuser. They then become even more demanding and difficult. Some have been known to ask if their spouse loves them or the children more. No healthy parent sees their own children as competition for attention. This lack of a constant supply of affirmation by their spouse is often used as a justification for bad behaviors by the psychological abuser. They say things like, "You're not meeting my needs," or "I am not your number one priority anymore," or "All you care about are the kids." These accusations against a survivor spouse can cause the survivor to question themselves as both a spouse and a parent. The psychological abuser has put the survivor in an impossible situation: meet the demands of the abuser or neglect their children. No parent should ever be put in the middle between their spouse and child.

Sometimes people will try to justify toxic behaviors in a marriage or partnership by saying things such as, "All couples have problems." The issue with this sort of comparison between a normal and an abusive relationship is that conflict in normal relationships do not leave the survivor spouse chronically lonely, lacking in relational nurturing, worried about how the abuse will affect their children, and needing to find restoration in key areas of their life. Yes, every couple will have their unique set of challenges, but not to the point of qualifying as being abusive. Toxic people like to try and normalize their actions. A statement about all couples having problems is an attempt to make the survivor feel like she or he is overreacting and being too sensitive. It is a diversion tactic to get the focus off of them—as the abuser—and on the survivor's reactions to the abuse.

### The Toxic Friend

Friendships are at the core of our regular support. They enrich our lives in numerous ways. Our friends are the family members we get to choose. Since friends have such personal access to us and our private thoughts, choosing wisely is critically important. We all have had a friendship where we wondered why we let that particular person close to us. I truly believe all personal growth is hindered (or completely ruined) by one of two things: 1) our own inner dialogue, and 2) the attitude of the people with whom we surround ourselves on a regular basis. Psychological abuse among peers can be widely missed under the guise that all friends challenge one another. We can get confused by whether a person is being honest or offensive. The difference between a normal friendship, with ups and downs, and an abusive one lies within the impact it has on the survivor. The intentions of the toxic person are also key to identifying friendship abuse.

*Venomous friends will not adhere to boundaries set by other people.*

Venomous friends will not adhere to boundaries set by other people. They repeatedly push right past any off-limits signs you might have established. Example? It can play out when a survivor requests that a toxic person not include them in gossiping about others. The psychologically abusive friend will completely ignore the request and continue to drag the survivor into drama. These folks also often like to be the expert of other people's lives. They know how to raise kids better, how to be better Christians, or basically how to accomplish anything with more success. They do it all so well, and if only the silly people around them would watch and learn. Of course that last sentence is oozing with sarcasm, but that really is how toxic friends think. Some will even go so far as to tell you that they are overwhelmed because their lives are "perfect." Yes. They do say such ridiculous statements out loud, for others to hear. It is bizarre they cannot hear themselves.

## The Group of Abusers

A group of toxic people come in different shapes and sizes. They can be a family, a group of church members, or a cluster of co-workers. One of the common themes of a toxic group is the fact that they do not want to get to know the real survivor. They want to construct a false image of the person so it justifies the abusive behaviors by the perpetrators. It is the classic setup of creating a scapegoat, and the survivor taking the brunt of the collective dysfunction of the group.

## *The Toxic Family*

The hateful and stinging words of a psychologically abusive parent can linger in the mind of an adult
child long after the adult has left home. This is because
narcissists, sociopaths, and psychopaths make terrible
parents. They lack the basic empathy and selfless nature
that loving parenting requires. They have no problem
meeting their own needs before their child's needs, and
feel completely justified in their actions. Abusers create
valid resentments. Later in life, they wonder why they
have no authentic relationship with their adult child.
Chronic selfishness and parenting do not go together.

Bonded relationships are not the goal in toxic families. Siblings often will be pitted against each other. This is
done so toxic parents maintain control over the
relationships within the family, even when the siblings
are adults. The triangulation may be overt or subtle, but
the damage to the attachments among family members
is still fully accomplished. It may be hard to imagine a
parent who sabotages close relationships among their
children, but I have been witness to abusive households
where they produced siblings who were in constant turmoil with one another. There is a clinical term called
"pseudomutality," and it relates to many harmful families.
The word describes those relatives who appear to have
some level of connection and agreement, but in fact, have
very dysfunctional and harmful relationships behind
the public image. The façade presented to the world is a
close-knit family, but the reality is a shallow and destruc-

tive unit.

Toxic families can find strength in their numbers. The larger the extended family, the more successful the depths of dysfunction are hidden, especially from outsiders. Toxic families use a number of abusive techniques to accomplish several wanted outcomes. Some family members will utilize the silent treatment to show their lack of regard, and have no problem doing so even to grandchildren. They can also use the "Us versus Them" philosophy regarding relatives and non-related spouses or significant others. Some toxic families may use excessive gossip to create tension among individuals. Recognizing the abuse and not personalizing the dysfunction is one of the first steps towards recovery. If you observe a toxic family long enough, you will see that their focus can shift from one scapegoated member to another. Psychologically abusive families can never be without a targeted victim. Otherwise, they would have to look at their own individual issues and deal with them. That is not likely to happen.

*Psychologically abusive families can never be without a targeted victim. Otherwise, they would have to look at their own individual issues and deal with them. That is not likely to happen.*

Psychologically abusive families like to use a divide and conquer technique. They especially love to use it within the in-law relationships. Have you ever known a family where the mother-in-law had issues with the wives of her sons? Perhaps it was the opposite? The son-in-law is the targeted family member. The way divide and conquer is used within a toxic family system is often very covert; it will look innocent, but be assured it is not done out of naivety. Example? Abusive family members will physically try to divide their family member away from the targeted in-law spouse. It can look as simple as not leaving room in the car for the in-law so she or he is forced to ride separate from their spouse. It might include the extended family all walking into a restaurant, and "conveniently" there is room at the long table for the family member—and even their children—to sit together, but all the surrounding seats are quickly filled by the toxic family members. This leaves the in-law spouse to find a seat at the end of the table, away by themselves from his or her spouse and their children. Divide and conquer.

The goal of this sort of abuse is to make the in-law feel rejected, unwelcomed, and left out of the extended family. The in-law's spouse and even children are in the family "club" but not the isolated, targeted in-law. It is the adult version of grade-school mean girl (or mean boy) games. How well do you think the in-law's complaints will be received? The survivor ends up being called disagreeable, insecure, and controlling. That is not the case at all. In the depths of their souls, they feel the hidden games that are being played. Psychological abuse is often very covert, so it does come out sounding petty to complain about sitting away from their spouse and children when at a restaurant with the toxic extended family. That is exactly how the abusive family members want it. They purposefully construct situations where the in-law will end up looking ridiculous because of their angry, sad, or emotionally charged responses to the covert abuse that is present, but hidden.

Abusive families function like Venus flytraps. They are a carnivorous predator that lure small creatures to come close with its pleasant features. Once the plant senses it has a live insect or spider on its surface, the plant snaps shut, and traps the creature inside. That is when it starts to literally digest its prey. Disgusting. Toxic families are no different. They lure members to stay in a dysfunctional and abusive environment by using pleasant things as enticements. Money is often one of the levers that is pulled. Promises (and sometimes follow through) to pay for vacations, pay off mortgages, buy cars, and pay for college for grandkids are a few of the most popular lures I have seen used by toxic families. Another carrot dangled is obligation. Some harmful families love to throw around all of their needs, and they have no regard for the survivor. The survivor is made to feel obligated to meet the demands (both spoken and unspoken) of the narcissists, sociopaths, and psychopaths on their family tree. Obligation is a powerful driver when we are raised in environments that teach us to ignore our safety and well-being. Who wants to prove an abuser right by acting selfishly and not showing up for family in times of need? But how exactly are selfishness

*Psychologically abusive people can only maintain normalcy for short spurts of time. Being an authentically caring, decent person isn't baseline for them. They must fake the behaviors that would show these positive character qualities. These fraudulent acts of kindness have brief shelf lives before they expire and the abusers return to their normal state of affairs.*

or need defined? Abusive families have a knack for stirring up drama just so they can have the spotlight of attention and appear needy. It's hard to know which is a real necessity and not a manufactured one.

The second step of the Venus flytrap family occurs once the lure (e.g., money) is successful. It is then that the poison starts dripping again. Psychologically abusive people can only maintain normalcy for short spurts of time. Being an authentically caring, decent person isn't baseline for them. They must fake the behaviors that would show these positive character qualities. These fraudulent acts of kindness have brief shelf lives before they expire and the abusers return to their normal state of affairs. I believe the hard swing back to their typical personality disordered selves is usually much worse after a time of counterfeit niceness.

They entice wounded family members in for much needed loving attention, but the family members once again find themselves beaten up and rejected. The repeated nature of abuse is what makes family abuse incredibly hard to break away from and to find lasting recovery. Who doesn't want to be loved by their family? Who wakes up in the morning just hoping their relatives will say and do horrible things to them? No one. Belonging is at the core of our human experience. We are hardwired to need and want to be included. Everyone desires to know that we have people and that our people have us. It is this exact human necessity abusers exploit for gain.

A survivor who is isolated (whether in physical or emotional distance) from his or her family of origin will experience profound grieving. A survivor who is abused, mocked, and shamed by in-laws might deal with grieving, but most likely will identify with feeling anger. When our extended families or in-laws don't love us the way we deserve as human beings, life does change. Holidays are altered. Life milestones are often awkward. Tension is present instead of warmth and attachment. Healing from toxic families is a slow journey because survivors are having to rewire deeply held beliefs. Recovery is absolutely possible. Survivors give their healing a huge boost when they understand that personal restoration from family abuse takes time.

## *The Toxic Church: Its Leadership and Members*

Why is it that a lot of people are cautious about things that have to do with Christianity? I think it's because there are far too many pastors and ministry leaders out there running amok in the name of God. They are doing a lot of harm in the process—damaging people who are trying to find God in the blur of modern life. Let me pause here and be clear that I am not saying all pastors or ministry leaders are awful. I am saying some, if not many, are miserable examples of the wonderful character qualities of love, patience, kindness, and hope. I have been a part of churches and ministries for over 20 years. I have seen the best and the worst Christianity has to offer.

Many people still believe all narcissists, sociopaths, and psychopaths are overtly grandiose and obvious in their toxic behaviors. After spending decades immersed in church culture, I can assure you not all psychological abusers are outwardly grandiose. In a religious setting, the appearance of humility is highly regarded, and grandiosity would be frowned upon. Therefore, toxic people hiding in church communities will take on the mannerisms and communication patterns of those around them. These psychological abusers do not fit the standard image. The normal teachings of how to spot a personality disordered person do not apply. We must become educated as to the various personas toxic people can manifest in order to hide their abusive behaviors.

Some narcissists, sociopaths, and psychopaths will

use calculated efforts to befriend pastors and church leaders in order to create a public persona that can hide the truth that they are a psychological abuser. Church leadership would be wise to watch for inconsistencies in people's stories, and not ignore red flags that are present. When church leadership fails, or flat out refuses, to recognize abusive people, the leaders are further abusing survivors by omission. I have watched abusive individuals be allowed to serve in leadership roles when the fruit in their lives did not show a healthy relationship with God or their families. Psychological abusers are often allowed to hold positions of authority in churches, and the family members are never interviewed to find out if the person is living an authentic life behind closed household doors. Far too many churches are believing the notion that if it looks good, it must be good. Nowhere does fake billboard living work with more efficiency than in a church environment. Leaders must gain better discernment in order to have the wisdom to sift through who is a fraud and who is authentic.

*Far too many churches are believing the notion that if it looks good, it must be good. Nowhere does fake billboard living work with more efficiency than in a church environment.*

There has been a trend towards some toxic church leaders and congregation members using "shunning" as a form of punishment towards individuals, couples, and even families. Why? The Scripture about not associating with the unrepentant is being twisted to justify psychologically abusing people by withholding relationship and support. Rather than being restoration focused, these toxic leaders and members are primarily concerned with maintaining control over people, and keeping their constructed public image untarnished. Shunning is being used against healthy people who simply dare to speak out about a powerful narcissistic, sociopathic, or psychopathic leader or member. In many situations, it is not being used merely for the "safety" of the congregation, as the leaders tell people. It is a version of sweeping issues under the proverbial rug and pretending the complaints are limited to a few "haters" of the church or ministry.

*When toxic church or ministry leaders feel threatened by the truth being revealed, they attack. The perfect target is the messenger of the truth. Those are typically people who were once close to the leaders, but fell out of good graces when they began asking the wrong (but actually correct) questions.*

When toxic church or ministry leaders feel threatened by the truth being revealed, they attack. The perfect target is the messenger of the truth. Those are typically people who were once close to the leaders, but fell out of good graces when they began asking the wrong (but actually correct) questions. Psychologically abusive leaders can be so well insulated by yes-men and yes-women, that to be questioned about their actions comes as a rude awakening. The individuals and couples who dare to stand up will be shunned out of the congregation community. The larger the congregation or ministry staff, the more well insulated a toxic leader will become. At some point, they are out of reach of any constructive criticism or exposure for abusive behaviors.

Men and women are being harmed in some churches and ministries. More attention needs to be focused on this area. Not so embarrassment can come to the collective Church, but so healing can happen. Harm in the name of God must be called out for what it is: Spiritual Abuse. This form of abuse occurs in many ways. The most common I have witnessed is the misapplied application of Scripture regarding forgiveness, divorce, and acceptance of intolerable behaviors. Not only are church leaders ill-prepared to recognize situations where one of the parties is personality disordered, but a common career path chosen by narcissists is that of the pastor. Survivors are receiving very poor "counseling" from ministry staff and volunteers who have no professional training in mental health. Church leaders cannot be expected to give informed advice regarding the type of abusive relationships that many therapists struggle to recognize and treat. Furthermore, toxic people are drawn to the ministry for the power that is unquestionably afforded to them. The veil must be pulled back to reveal what is currently hiding in the darkness of modern Christianity. When psychological abuse and spiritual abuse are present, many survivors find themselves questioning their faith as a result of the harmful actions perpetrated.

## The Toxic Workplace

Narcissists, sociopaths, and psychopaths have to earn a living. Guess where they end up? As employees, co-workers, managers, and senior level executives. Toxic people in the workplace often use very covert methods to undermine a survivor's success. This can look like chronically not giving survivors all the information needed to complete assignments, and then embarrassing them when the tasks are not done as they should have been. Sometimes the abuse is not covert but very overt and aggressive. Again, there are many ways psychological abusers can manifest their dysfunctions. Survivors have shared that they have been aggressively yelled at, publicly mocked, and even physically touched in a manner meant as an act of dominance. Regardless of how a survivor is experiencing the abuse, the toll it takes physically and emotionally can still be the same. The threat that comes from workplace abuse causes many survivors to experience overwhelming anxiety about going to work each day. The intensity may vary between situations, but chronically being harmed at work will begin to have a negative consequence on the survivor.

## *When* do psychological abusers harm others?

Abusers like to target people who have something they do not or cannot possess themselves. Narcissists, sociopaths, and psychopaths are notorious for picking targets that initially boost their egos. It could be the target's appearance, age, intellect, reputation, religious convictions, career success, family, friends, or something else.

Once the target is hooked, the toxic person then sets out to tear down the exact qualities that attracted her or him to the survivor in the first place. It is a source of power and entertainment for a toxic person to destroy an originally healthy and happy person. This point is often missed by survivors because in the middle of the abuse, they see themselves as

*It is a source of power and entertainment for a toxic person to destroy an originally healthy and happy person. This point is often missed by survivors because in the middle of the abuse, they see themselves as broken. Since the abuser says such hateful things, the survivor assumes they were targeted because they are "weak." That is the exact opposite of the truth.*

broken. Since the abuser says such hateful things, the survivor assumes they were targeted because they are "weak." That is the exact opposite of the truth. Targets who hold no value to abusers won't even be bothered with, and a bigger "prize" would have originally been found. Psychological abusers like people who make them look or feel good. Much like leeches, they attach themselves to people who give them sustenance of some sort. Once they have had their fill, the abuser will begin the process of destroying the qualities of the survivor that produce jealous feelings in the abuser. Since toxic people cannot possess certain positive attributes, they do not want the survivor to have them either.

Psychological abusers like to arrange everything and everyone right in the places that serve them best. Example? I often say that they have an imaginary chess board of their lives. They maneuver all of the pieces on the board exactly as it suits them to "win." Toxic people have very little to no regard for how their actions impact those around them. Survivors must come to recognize that their best interests will never be considered by a toxic person. A survivor must take steps to ensure a high-quality life for themselves. That plan may not fit into the psychological abuser's game of chess.

### How do psychological abusers harm others?

Toxic people are great actors. They will utilize whichever props are available to maintain control in the relationship. For example, some psychological abusers will use tears when it serves to make them look like the victim. They may also use outward expressions of emotions when needing to look like they have changed, but are actually attempting to manipulate the survivor back into the toxic game. Manipulative people use a wide range of fake emotions to try and control those around them.

*Toxic people are great actors. They will utilize whichever props are available to maintain control in the relationship.*

In addition to tears, they may use guilt in an effort to make a survivor feel badly for setting boundaries. A toxic person can utilize anger to intimidate people into being compliant. They may try to appear overly happy in an effort to make a survivor feel discarded and forgotten. The important point to remember is that most outwardly expressed emotions of psychological abusers are for a distinct purpose; that is usually to harm others in some way. Their actions cannot be trusted nor can they be taken at face value. Psychological abusers have perfected the use of their acting skills for a reason.

One of the most common things I hear from survivors is their confusion about why they did not notice the red flags sooner in the relationship. It doesn't matter if the toxic person is a parent, co-worker, friend, romantic interest, or religious leader. Almost all survivors seriously doubt themselves for not seeing the toxicity sooner. The common question is, "How did I let this happen to me?"

This form of abuse is difficult to specifically pinpoint, and that is what makes it so insidious. Abusers work hard to hide their true motives. They lie and shift the blame onto the survivors. In order for the pattern of abuse to be seen, survivors will experience many episodes that leave them deeply hurt. Psychological abuse is not a one-and-done type of harm. I often relate the process that survivors go through as "collecting pebbles." One pebble represents a single, negative encounter with a psychological abuser.

In the early stages of a relationship, there might be an awareness that something isn't quite right. A survivor will have a few pebbles in their fictional bag. The bag isn't very heavy and only holds a couple of weird or hurtful moments with the abuser. Certainly not enough evidence of toxicity to cut a family member from your life, quit a job, break up with a boyfriend/girlfriend, leave a church, and most definitely not enough to end a marriage. They are only a few negative moments, right? At this point, survivors will rationalize that nobody is perfect, and everyone has character defects. Good days and bad days. It is human nature to look at one, two, three, or four unpleasant moments with people and not take them too seriously. We often shrug off these moments and move on. Over time, recognizing the pebbles (hurtful moments) causes the bag to become very heavy—too heavy to carry anymore. Many survivors describe being crushed under the weight of the abuse and the chronic dysfunction of the abuser.

However, toxic people like to isolate one incident at a time. They argue that what they said, or did, was not that big of a deal. They want to deal with one pebble at a time and not look at the entire weight of the abuse. They accuse survivors of "focusing on the past" or they say things like, "The problem is that you won't forgive me for my mistakes." No, the problem is that psychological abusers keep making the same "mistakes" or choices to harm other people. They may want to focus on one incident at a time but it's impossible; just like one cannot separate out a single raindrop while in a thunderstorm. I chose the cover picture of the book for a few reasons. One of which is that the image of rain reminds me of the way psychological abusers inflict their harm, one drop of torture at a time.

Narcissists, sociopaths, and psychopaths typically have developed and sharpened their observation skills. This is how they systematically collect information about targets and use it later to the abuser's advantage. A psychological abuser will find a survivor's emotional soft spots and exploit them for control and entertainment. Example? A target might casually mention a personal weakness or insecurity. The toxic person will tuck the information away to be darted back at the survivor when the time suits the abuser. They are always collecting data to use as a tool of harming people. This is why, moving forward in recovery, a survivor's personal information must be divulged slowly and with the constant intent of protecting oneself. Learning to not be "all in" too soon in a relationship, but remain guarded, is usually an area of growth for many survivors. Being an immediate open book with personal information will always come back to bite.

Once a toxic person has enough information, they like to manipulate by throwing in small portions of the truth about the survivor. How? The two favorites are the truth about the survivor's insecurities, or the truth regarding the survivor's own areas of growth. Why do abusive people specifically highlight these two areas? They are trying to get the survivor to take all the blame for the conflict and relational issues. A spoonful of the truth makes their poison go down easier and less detected. Each one of us is more likely to believe someone when they point out our flaws and can connect what we know to be true about our character defects with their complaints of us. It is the perfect set up for the survivor to take the responsibility and allow the abuser to be completely off the hook.

> *Each one of us is more likely to believe someone when they point out our flaws and can connect what we know to be true about our character defects with their complaints of us. It is the perfect set up for the survivor to take the responsibility and allow the abuser to be completely off the hook.*

Almost all survivors go through a moment in recovery when they wonder if the abuser is "dumb" and doesn't know the pain they cause. They then flip and wonder if the abuser is aware and knows exactly what they do. Being able to answer the "are they dumb or are they aware?" question is critical to a survivor's recovery. Psychological abusers know when and where to turn off their manipulative games. They know precisely how to push all the right emotional buttons to get the target's frustrated response that the abuser craves. They know how to triangulate people and make themselves appear to be the victim. You tell me, does that sound like someone too "dumb" to know that their actions harm others? They know.

When a survivor tries to talk to a psychological abuser about their negative behaviors, a favorite maneuver of toxic people is to simply not reply. They say nothing. Complete silence. When a survivor asks why they didn't reply, the toxic person will spin the situation and say something like, "I am not going to argue with you." Can you see what just happened? The survivor was blamed for causing drama, or an argument, and the toxic person never addressed their behaviors. They will go to great lengths to never discuss their own actions. Psychologically abusive people know exactly the manipulation game they play, and they know it works. Why do you think they have no interest in changing their ways? They enjoy the power, control, entertainment, and the game playing. It leaves the abuser holding the puppet strings of those closest to them.

Narcissists, sociopaths, and psychopaths hate having a target point out the inconsistencies in their actions. Toxic people work hard to hide their chaos producing behaviors. They pride themselves on being in control and unaffected by anything or anyone. It is a lie though. They typically become defensive when a survivor starts recognizing the patterns of their actions. As a diversion tactic, an abuser may say things like, "My real friends are not mean to me," or "A good spouse would never act this way," or "I would expect more from a mature employee." These statements are meant to shift the spotlight away from the abuser's lack of consistency and onto the survivor. Psychological abusers do not take responsibility for their actions, so that must be flung onto someone else.

In order for the toxic person to shift the blame off of themselves and onto the survivor, they like to start sentences with the words, "If only..." If only the survivor wasn't sensitive, if only the survivor could be forgiving, if only the survivor wasn't jealous, then the relationship could be saved. Not true. "If only..." is a subtle form of abuse because it makes the abuser sound wishful that the relationship could be salvaged and healthier. In reality, they feed off the conflict. They have no desire for lasting relational attachments. Abusers get one more opportunity to covertly insult the survivor when they say, "If only..."

Toxic people like to accuse survivors of being selfish. This is often done when a survivor attempts something

46

good for himself or herself. The abuser wants to ruin the enjoyment of the activity. It is a calculated effort to keep a survivor exhausted, anxious, and confused. A survivor who practices self-care is a threat to a psychological abuser. Through caring for themselves, a survivor might gain enough inner-strength to set boundaries and refuse to live in fear. Limiting the amount of time a survivor can spend on activities that they enjoy is a form of a brainwashing technique. Our quality of life will be seriously impaired if we are withdrawn into isolation and lack moments of hope in our daily lives. By shaming the survivor as selfish for wanting to go do fun things—typically without the abuser—the survivor would have to push through an enormous amount of guilt in order to still find enjoyment. Prior to recovery, most survivors would simply not go do the fun activity, for fear of retribution by the abuser. Once in recovery, individuals see the game being played against them and refuse to be held back from creating a vibrant life.

*Our quality of life will be seriously impaired if we are withdrawn into isolation and lack moments of hope in our daily lives.*

Psychological abusers set people up for failure. They enjoy trying to prove a survivor wrong and embarrassing them. How is this accomplished? An abuser will give incorrect information, then stand back to watch the target take the bait (lie). They will mock, shame, and criticize the survivor for doing the "wrong" thing. This is done to bring further validity to any gossip the abuser has spread about the survivor, and to make themselves look like they are the true victim. Toxic people will go to elaborate lengths to set up a survivor. Abusers want to make the survivor look bad in the eyes of those observing. Normal people have a hard time comprehending that abusers go to such lengths, but they do. This disbelief is often a hindrance to outsiders seeing the harm being done. In order to see it, they must be willing to accept that some people are capable of evil and gain entertainment out of psychologically harming innocent people.

Toxic people are in a constant heightened alert to never look like anything is their fault. Example? They will lie and argue that they gave an apology when, in fact, they did not. When asked by a survivor why the abuser never took ownership for the hurt they caused, a psychological abuser might reply with, "I said I was sorry!" In reality, they never said those actual words. They argued about the facts of the situation or blamed the survivor. Perhaps both. Rarely does a toxic person give an authentic apology. To do so would be too much evidence that they are just like everyone else and flawed. Their delusional, grandiose self-image must be pro-

> *Rarely does a toxic person give an authentic apology. To do so would be too much evidence that they are just like everyone else and flawed.*

tected. They fight to maintain the illusion that they are always correct. If any apology is ever given, a survivor must really listen to see if the abuser is saying a version of an apology that somehow serves the abuser, is using a circular conversation communication style to confuse the survivor, or both tactics. Authentic, lasting remorse is not in a psychological abuser's skill set.

Psychological abusers will adamantly deny that their actions are hurtful. Survivors can spend excessive amounts of time trying to explain precisely what the toxic person has done that is abnormal. The abuser may even temporarily admit their actions are harmful, but what always follows is the hard swing back to their baseline of denial. Abusers like to say things like, "What do I do to you?" or "How do I make your life harder?" These comments come even after the survivor has spent hours laying out all the evidence of abuse. The bottom line? Psychological abusers will never take lasting responsibility for their behaviors. It is incredibly fruitless for survivors to continue to try to get the abuser to see their actions. They will never admit to seeing it because they already know what they do, and choose to continue in their selfish harmful ways.

One of the main allegations that narcissists, sociopaths, and psychopaths make against survivors is that they accuse survivors of being disrespectful. Why is this complaint so common for toxic people? It is because their grossly over-inflated egos make them believe that even the most minor correction, or disagreement, with

*Survivors are wise to not fall into the trap of second guessing all of their actions because it is likely they could never show enough agreement to please a truly toxic person.*

the toxic person's opinion is a huge sign of disrespect. Survivors are wise to not fall into the trap of second guessing all of their actions because it is likely they could never show enough agreement to please a truly toxic person. Survivors in recovery come to realize that just because an abuser says the survivor's actions are disrespectful, it does not mean it is true. Even the most non-confrontational discussions can be twisted on the survivor. Only in the mind of a psychological abuser does a regular conversation of sharing opinions equate to disrespect. They live in their own distorted worlds where they are king and queen of all opinions.

## Why do Psychological Abusers Harm Others?

I do a lot of reading, listening to podcasts, and radio shows on the topic of narcissism, sociopathy, psychopathy, and the recovery from this type of abuse. I can tell you there are different camps of people out there who propose a wide range of beliefs about the development of personality disorders. Some argue that there is a spectrum of what we should expect as normal human character flaws. Narcissism seems to be the gray area where most discord bubbles up. Common teachings on sociopaths and psychopaths center on their intense lack of empathy. Hollywood has even attempted to paint a picture of how people with personality disorders behave. Some of these characters are true reflections of the disorders, and some are merely Hollywood attempts at making an exciting movie or television show.

Let me stop here and correct a very common misconception: personality disorders are not the same classification of mental health disorders, such as Bipolar Disorder or Major Depressive Disorder. Recently, I was horrified to read a blog post that was completely misguided about the true nature of the "disorder" part of narcissistic and anti-social disorders. The poorly written article went so far as to say survivors who insist narcissists, sociopaths, and psychopaths be held accountable for their abusive actions are actually discriminating against disordered people. Yes, they went there. What utter nonsense. It does highlight the lack of true understanding that gets slogged around online and paraded as truth. Personality disorders are in a different category in the DSM5 (the diagnostic manual used by therapists to diagnose clients) than other organic mental health issues.

People are not born personality disordered, but people can be born with Bipolar Disorder or Autism. Both of those diagnoses are in the DSM5. Personality disorders are created during childhood and adolescence through a lack of healthy attachments to their primary caregivers. These

*Personality disorders are created during childhood and adolescence through a lack of healthy attachments to their primary caregivers.* attachments can be through extreme and repetitive over-indulgence where normal societal rules did not apply to the child and then as a teenager. It is the environment where caregivers chronically covered up for the youth. These individuals came to see others as only a source of making life easier for them. Having a one-sided relationship was the norm. The overindulged child and teenager learned that people are there not as a source of mutual enjoyment.

Instead, they are to be used for their own gain. It is not "helicopter parenting," but rather it is a severe lack of boundaries—failing to remind the youth that he or she is one of millions of people in the world. The parental message was that the child and teen are unique, special, and beyond the rules that lowly, normal people must follow. This message wasn't delivered just once and the child became toxic. It encompassed the child's entire upbringing and bled into adulthood. Through the chronic choices of the now personality disordered adult, the lack of attachment patterns from childhood continue.

On the other side of that experience, a lack of true attachment can occur through emotional neglect during childhood and then teen years. Their physical needs could have been met, but there may have been other forms of neglect that included fake connections that ran deep within the family unit. This history could cause some people to pause and feel bad for the personality disordered person, but please do not. Many individuals grew up in homes that were not loving and yet, they have maintained high levels of empathy and care for other people. Toxic individuals who did not have caregivers meet their need for authentic attachment decided once they were old enough to meet their own needs, it became a game of "getting mine" at all costs. These folk also have developed a high level of entitlement, but not because they were raised that way. They view life as owing them, and their insatiable appetite causes them to want more of whatever other people have to offer. They use individuals with no regard for the well-being of those involved. They are infamous "takers" in a sea of "givers" in their lives. As long as they get theirs, who cares?

Regardless of how the lack of attachment came to be part of the abuser's personality, the truth is they continue to sustain their harmful behaviors through free will. Many people grew up in homes that did not meet their needs or were overindulgent to the point of dysfunctional. People come into adulthood with all sorts of misconceptions from their childhoods. They must rewire these beliefs in order to have healthy adult lives. This includes having good relationships and quality parenting. Countless individuals seek out self-help books, seminars, counseling, and other opportunities to heal and grow from their upbring-

*Countless individuals seek out self-help books, seminars, counseling, and other opportunities to heal and grow from their upbringing. Why can't narcissists, sociopaths, and psychopaths do the same thing? They will not simply because they have so thoroughly convinced themselves there is absolutely nothing wrong with them. Nothing.*

ing. Why can't narcissists, sociopaths, and psychopaths do the same thing? They will not simply because they have so thoroughly convinced themselves there is absolutely nothing wrong with them. Nothing. They may give lip service to some of their supposed faults, but their actions do not back up the statements that they have issues to be dealt with and permanently fixed. Any self-awareness they may exhibit is short-lived at best, and true therapeutic work is never sustained. The bottom line: these individuals do not want to change. The way they live their lives works for them, and why wouldn't it? It's all about them. Everything seems to boomerang back to their needs, their wants, their time, their goals; their, their, their. It gets very old for survivors to always live in the shadows of their demands and their expectations.

There is a huge difference between having character defects that must be dealt with and exhibiting the qualities of a personality disordered person. At any given moment, do we all have the ability to be completely self-serving, act manipulatively, be snarky to a stranger, snap at our kids, slam doors in the middle of an adult temper tantrum, or seek our own self-preservation at the expense of someone else? Sure we do. No one would argue people can be real dirtbags at times. However, once the moment of our "toddler-esque" meltdown is over, we feel bad. We realize what jerks we were and are embarrassed that we took our inner annoyances out on other people. We apologize by telling them we're sorry, doing something nice for them, or we inwardly repent for being hostile towards others. We come back to our baseline of being normally empathetic human beings who can reflect on our ridiculous behaviors. Narcissists cannot do that. Sociopaths and psychopaths cannot do that. They cannot, will not, and do not desire to be self-reflective. They will always blame others and will never, ever change. Why would they? In their own eyes, it is everyone else who is deeply flawed and require fixing.

# COMMON CHARACTER TRAITS
## OF SURVIVORS

We have spent some time looking at who, what, where, when, how, and why psychological abuse occurs. I want to pause and talk briefly about what I have noticed in the survivors of this type of abuse. Targets of hidden abuse seem to have a few important and common character qualities. Some are positive, and some definitely need to be managed.

Being highly adaptable is one of those positive traits. Many survivors will describe her or his pre-abuse core personality as one that could "make lemonade out of lemons." Before the abuse, survivors were frequently said to be easy-going, able to shake off setbacks, and to stay hopeful. It is often the ability to bounce back after a stressful season that abusers exploit in survivors. Abusers push and push, waiting for the survivors to break emotionally. If not managed, being resilient to chaos can definitely be both a blessing and a curse. Does this sound familiar to you? Has your own strength been used as a weapon against you?

People have some confusion about what type of person is drawn into a psychologically abusive relationship. The stereotype is that victims of any form of abuse must be needy, dependent individuals who are unable to function without constant reassurance from their abusers. This is absolutely not true. Most survivors of hidden abuse never imagined they would come to doubt themselves in the intense way they did during the toxic connection. One of the main steps of healing is to come to terms with how much their core personhood changed while in the harmful environment.

Often it is asked if being codependent and being an Empath (highly empathetic person) are the same things. No, they are not. How are they different? Codependency involves an unhealthy enmeshment that occurs between two people. It usually happens in relationships where one person enables the other individual to make poor choices. People who struggle with codependency can learn new ways of thinking and behaving. Being an Empath is a personality type, and it has many beautiful qualities.

> *Boundaries are the foundation for regulating a high degree of compassion for other people.*

Like any set of character traits, there will be pros and cons. People who identify as being highly empathetic will benefit from learning how to keep their levels of empathy from becoming harmful to their well-being.

Boundaries are the foundation for regulating a high degree of compassion for other people. Psychological abusers exploit the exact traits that most empaths find beautiful in themselves. In recovery, many survivors begin to self-identify as being highly empathetic. They see that their relationship strengths were used against them by the abuser.

One of the most common character traits I have witnessed among survivors is their ability and desire to be self-reflective. As a generalization, most survivors are able to critically look at their own behaviors and motives. They are willing to fix character defects within themselves. These personal strengths are precisely what narcissists, sociopaths, and psychopaths exploit. A toxic person knows if they hurl accusations at a survivor, those words will pierce deep. They cause the survivor to look inward to reflect on whether the complaints against them are true. Quite the clever diversion tactic. It is the psychological abuser who needs to do more self-reflection, but that will never, ever, happen.

Toxic environments bring out poor behaviors in even the most patient of individuals. Survivors of psychological abuse find themselves behaving in ways that don't fit their normal personality. This shift can serve as a red flag that the environment is unhealthy. The change in survivors can sadly also fuel any toxic gossip being spread by abusive individuals or groups of people. Example? An abuser does something exceptionally hurtful and the spotlight is on him or her. The survivor reacts with anger, and guess where that spotlight is now? On the survivor. It should remain on the abuser for their actions that started the tension, but the survivor's reaction is what gets all the attention. It is a vicious cycle that allows toxic people to repeatedly shift the blame away from themselves. Survivors regain their feelings of self-worth when they take control by either having No Contact or through Detached Contact and creating plans to deal with the triggers unhealthy environments can produce. If you have found yourself acting in ways that seem to add to the constant list of complaints by the abuser, take heart. You are, or were, doing the best you could with the knowledge you had at the time. As we move into the six stages of recovery, the intent is to increase your understanding about what you have been through. In doing so, you will also find new levels of awareness.

Some survivors of psychological abuse find themselves taking on a few of the negative traits of an abuser. How? A survivor may use the silent treatment (abruptly stopping communication and giving no responses) to punish. The survivor does this because the silent treatment was a weapon against them and it hurt deeply. The target is trying to show the abuser how devastating silence can be, but it is a wasted effort on behalf of the survivor. An abuser will not change her or his ways merely by having the tables turned on them. In their mind, they are justified for the actions they take against others. The double standard is that abusers do not believe they deserve to be treated poorly. A survivor is far better off to remain loyal to their true self and create a healthy distance from the abuser.

When survivors share specific details of a psychologically abusive encounter, many start their sentences with something like, "I know it sounds stupid" or "I know it is not a big deal, but…" They then go on to share incidents that perfectly highlight the cryptic and hidden nature of psychological abuse. By itself, each toxic conversation or moment may not mean a lot. However, when a survivor starts to string them all together, the pervasive pattern of life always centering on the abuser becomes crystal clear. It is not unlike those pictures that are made up of hundreds of little dots. Sure, you could get really close and focus your eyes on just one dot but that does not show you very much. If you took the dots—or moments of psychologically abusive behaviors—in their totality, what would you see? What painting has been created by the abuser? Probably not something you would want to hang on the wall to look at every day. This is precisely why recovery is needed.

Recognizing psychological abuse can be tricky because depending on the angle that you view the behaviors, they can change from abusive to normal. How? When a toxic person uses the silent treatment to punish, a survivor could choose to incorrectly re-frame the abusive behavior as merely the other person not wanting to argue, or needing some temporary space from the tension. Psychological abusers count on a target to minimize and normalize their toxic behaviors, and be willing to take more abuse. Survivors do themselves a huge favor when they do not make excuses for harmful actions. An important question for targets: Would you treat someone the way you've been treated? If the answer is no, then the abuse is easier to recognize. Resist remaining in any level of denial. The truth is painful to see, but necessary.

# SIX STAGES OF RECOVERY

# STAGE ONE: DESPAIR

*When survivors first begin counseling for psychological abuse recovery, many don't even know they have been abused. They do know life has become unmanageable, and they are looking for answers. Some don't yet understand the full depth of what has been done to them by the abuser(s). At the beginning of counseling, survivors are (more times than not) in emotional chaos, anxious, depressed, or suicidal. Sometimes all of the above and more. The very first place we start is their safety to not harm themselves. Once that has been established, we begin the work of identifying the despair the survivor feels. The first stage of recovery can be a scary season in life. Luckily, several more stages follow, and hope begins to shine through.*

One of the first things I must do with my new clients is assess the risk of them harming themselves. Let me be blunt here: as a therapist, I have to determine if I think a new client might try to kill himself or herself. Sometimes psychological abuse can become so life altering, survivors sink into serious depths of depression. They don't yet know they have been a puppet on strings and skillfully played by an abusive puppet-master. They just recognize they cannot continue to live how they have been and that is the truth. However, suicide must not be the answer. Ever. I am going to pause here and say that if you have found yourself scared of any thoughts or feelings you have had about possibly harming yourself, please do what I ask my clients to do, which is to be honest with someone. Tell a friend, a therapist, call 911, or go to your nearest emergency room and get help. There are many things that can happen to lift people out of the pit of suicidal thoughts. I want you to get the care you need. If one person harms themselves because of an abuser, a deep ache runs through the recovery community. We are all in this journey together.

Once I can determine a new client is not at risk for self-harm, we then begin the work of identifying despair that the survivor feels. We start unraveling what exactly has happened to him or her. No two stories of psychological abuse will be exactly the same, but there are some incredibly familiar themes. Later on in *Chapter Two: Education*, you will see how survivor stories are similar in some ways. As I said before, advocates in the recovery community often joke that there must be some toxic person manual out there because it seems like they have all learned the same dirty tricks and games to play on unsuspecting people.

As I begin working with a new client, I usually ask

why she or he is looking for counseling, with me or another therapist. I always throw in the part about working with someone else because I do not assume I am a good fit for every client. If I did, I might need to look at whether or not I have some grandiose thinking. Rapport and seeing life through a similar lens are two very important components when a client and a therapist decide to work together. I also do not begin a therapeutic relationship with all the folks who make an appointment. The first session is helpful to see if we are going to be a good philosophical and personality fit. If not, I am always happy to give a referral to another therapist in town whom I know and trust. If you have met with a therapist and it didn't work for you, keep looking. Walking through the process of healing from psychological abuse is a very complex journey, so try not to go it alone if possible. There are great online resources for peer support. Part of my hope in writing this book is to start a movement of local peer-led book study groups. Survivors will be able to enjoy meeting one another as they work through the six stages of recovery in a safe environment. If you are interested in hosting or finding a local book study group, please visit www.healingfromhiddenabuse.com.

When a new client and I first meet, I ask a lot of questions. I am notorious for interrupting. The first time I do it in a session, I immediately apologize and explain that I have to stop the conversation every so often so I can look for the patterns within the situation the client is describing. If a client continues on with the story without pausing to hear what he or she is saying, the hidden nature of psychological abuse is surely missed. One of the reasons this form of abuse is so insidious is because pulling normal relationship issues (a non-toxic relationship) apart from that of an abusive relationship is often as close as bone is to marrow. At first glance, most toxic encounters look normal. Discord among co-workers, family members, friends, and loved ones happen. No one would argue that point. However, the therapeutic work begins when we are able to sift out the relationship junk that is normal from the relationship abuse that turns a survivor's world upside down.

Most survivors of abuse who decide to come for counseling are pretty worn out when they arrive at my office. There is a wide range to the *Despair* stage. It runs from being confused as to why they have been treated the way they have, all the way to needing immediate medical care to help emotionally and/or physically stabilize. Those are the two polar ends, and most people land somewhere in the middle. What is common among all survivors is they will mentally replay conversations and situations concerning the abuser. They are looking for reasons why they were treated so badly. The confusion that comes with psychological abuse is one of the hardest to grasp. I often hear things like, "Something isn't right with this person. I know I am not perfect, but I don't treat people like this, and normal people don't act this way." That is correct. Normal people don't play all the toxic games psychological abusers do, and yet, survivors end up initially blaming themselves. The ultimate of sad irony.

While in the *Despair* stage, survivors of psychological abuse wonder what is wrong with them. They ask questions like, "Why can't I fix myself so this relationship will work?" "Why am I not strong enough to get over this?" and "Why am I such a broken mess?" Those are exactly the types of self-doubting and self-loathing questions abusers love. Why? Because survivors who are hating themselves are too busy to notice who the real problem is and make changes. Smoke and mirrors. That's how toxic people like it. They then have free reign to subversively wreak their havoc on the world around them.

Survivors who repeatedly believe they are the problem, they are broken, and they are not good enough, are people who are never going to see the hidden abuse. Not because they don't want to, but because they are looking in the wrong spot for answers. In therapy, we start to literally deprogram the conscious and subconscious lies the abusers have planted in the survivors. This is not unlike folks who have found themselves involved in cults. Deprogramming from psychological abuse is a necessary step that cannot be taken lightly or missed. Other-

> *In therapy, we start to literally deprogram the conscious and subconscious lies the abusers have planted in the survivors.*

wise, the lies will continue to run around in a survivor's internal dialogue, and keep her or him mentally trapped long after the contact with the abuser has ended. This is true whether the abuser was a family member, someone in the workplace, a peer, or religious leader. The recovery from psychological abuse always involves the survivor identifying the lies that have been told and seeing those lies as manipulation tools. What lies have you had to identify in your own abusive relationship?

A week does not go by that I don't hear at least one person say during a counseling session, "I can't do this anymore." I think these words are powerful. They should serve as an early warning system that change in some form is probably on the horizon, or at least it should be. An overload on *emotional capacity* is the reason people get to the point where they feel they cannot continue to stay in a relationship, remain at the same place of employment, continue in a one-sided friendship, struggle with the pressures created by a harmful spouse, try to meet unrealistic toxic family obligations, or whatever else might be at the core of an "I can't do this anymore" statement. Emotional capacity. We all have it in varying degrees, and it influences our ability to continue down a path that isn't best suited for us. If we have a high level of emotional capacity, it predisposes us to stay in abusive environments longer. That is not a great thing. On the other hand, a high level of emotional capacity helps survivors heal and truly recover. Our own strengths can be double-edged swords when dealing with abusive individuals.

Getting to the point of feeling like we can't continue doing something is not a bad thing. I have repeatedly watched amazingly strong men and women make some significant and needed life changes after they were able to get to their own "I can't do this anymore" point. This is why *Stage One* of recovery is called *Despair*. A deep sorrow is often how *Stage One* is described. A soul sorrow. A level of exhaustion that is at times hard to explain. If you have experienced it, you know what it feels like deep within you. No amount of sleep can touch a weary and bruised soul.

The challenge to *Stage One* is knowing whether we have really arrived at a point of true despair and change will come, or if it's just a temporary low point. Will we be heading back for more rounds of the same abuse (just a different month or year)? Just because we may be capable of forcing ourselves to continue down a certain path does not mean our nervous systems or physical health will be okay with that decision. I strongly believe in the mind-body connection, and if we continue doing what is harmful to us, our well-being will suffer at some point. It is inevitable. I have witnessed the full spectrum of client emotional and physical breakdowns due

*Just because we may be capable of forcing ourselves to continue down a certain path does not mean our nervous systems or physical health will be okay with that decision.*

to psychological abuse. I can share with you that once the body starts to shut down, a survivor must decide for whom and what they are living. Some abusers on the middle-to-high end of the toxicity spectrum have absolutely no reservations about damaging survivors in any way possible, even to their complete destruction.

As a therapist, I am probably known for being direct. I don't beat around the bush and refuse to shy away from the hard conversations. One question I have asked many folks is, "Are you going to choose yourself or your abuser?" The honest answer for most people in *Stage One* is they don't know, and guess what? That's okay. *Stage One* is not the time for making any big decisions. Most breaks in contact that survivors initiate during this stage do not last. They find themselves running right back to their relationship. That's okay, too. I am a big believer in not making lasting decisions until we know for sure they are the right decisions. Otherwise, we end up voicing idle threats and falling short on our follow-through. For the psychological abuser, this back-and-forth from the survivor only fuels their belief that they have the survivor firmly and completely under control. Being on the short emotional leash of an abuser can—and will—change even the strongest of people.

Many times I have watched a survivor describe her or his "old self," and the person sitting before me is only capable of showing tiny glimmers of that pre-abuse person. Some don't show any glimmers, and are fully entrenched in their current suffering. In a nutshell, the *Despair* stage is not pretty. It is the stage where the survivor realizes careers have been lost because of the chaos the abuser has brought into the survivor's life. It is the stage where some clients need hospitalization to find physical and/or emotional stability. For some, it is an intensely lonely stage because on the outside no one knows the raging pain going on inside. Some survivors do an exceptionally good job of hiding their brokenness from being involved in a psychologically abusive relationship. They hold it in and let no one know. That's the party line toxic people love most because an isolated victim is a controlled victim. For many people, coming to counseling is the only time they share what is really going on in their lives. I take the privilege to know the truth with tremendous humility and gratitude.

There are many reasons why a survivor might need to hide his or her wounds from the outside world. It could be because she or he is married to someone well-known in the community, and if the abuse is discovered, the social implications are very clear. Who is going to believe that a parent who is horrendous behind the walls of their home is the same person the general public thinks is a saint? How many people are going to believe that psychological abusers are also church leaders and pastors? Why bother saying anything since no one is going to take it seriously? There are survivors who are not willing to throw in the towel on their hard-earned, well-established careers, even though they are being emotionally hijacked while at work. They put their game face on every day and push through their despair.

For whatever reason you might find yourself in the first stage of recovery (*Despair*), the important part is you are starting. Many recovery programs believe in a one-day-at-a-time motto, and I am a huge advocate of this type of thinking. For today. That's it. For today, what can you do to put one foot in front of the other? For today, which decisions need to be made to help bring a little bit of order to your life? Just a little bit, mind you. No one is expecting perfection from you, so please do yourself a favor and try to resist the need to rush the healing process. Just like a physical wound, if we create the right environment and not pick at the wound, it will heal well on its own. Emotional healing is really no different. As we walk together through the remaining five stages of recovery, we will be creating the right environment for your healing. Little by little, not one big step forward, only to see you slide back to the starting point.

Stop right here and go take a look at a measuring stick. Find one in that junk drawer we all have, or pull up a picture of one on your cell phone. Got it? As you look at the measuring stick, remember we are not going from 1 inch to 12 inches all at once. While in *Stage One: Despair*, we are looking for growth on the little black lines of the measuring stick. Making changes, one small step at a time, will move a survivor from *Despair* down the line to *Stage Six: Maintenance*. Many before you have traveled this exact same journey. You are not alone. Can you do the same thing they have done? Of course you can, and you will if you are willing to slowly work towards the goal of healing. There are many underlying messages we must unravel, and a slow, steady pace is our best option.

At some point in counseling, almost every survivor of psychological abuse will ask me the question, "How do you know I am not the toxic one?" It's a legitimate question, but it also shows the level of self-doubt left after hidden abuse. My answer? A therapist who is familiar with this form of harm will listen closely to the stories the survivor tells and see the abusive patterns in voicemail messages, e-mails and/or text exchanges between the abuser and the survivor. It becomes very clear which one is the perpetrator of twisting the facts and creating chaos. The subtle nature of psychological abuse leaves survivors doubting themselves, but confidence is found in the healing process.

*The subtle nature of psychological abuse leaves survivors doubting themselves, but confidence is found in the healing process.*

In the early stages of recovery, survivors often talk about the toxic person as being "two completely different people." The survivor discusses the individual as if they are talking about a nice person and an abusive person. The real challenge with this approach is that it disjoints reality. The toxic person is not a loving individual with an evil twin who shows up once in a while. They are the evil twin. Some of them also happen to have good moments when they are enjoyable.

Survivors must fight the desire to compartmentalize the toxic person's behaviors and see them in their totality as one individual who is harmful to the survivor's well-being. The nice moments are often very confusing and cause the survivor's recovery to be delayed. I am not asking survivors to focus on the negative or remain bitter. I am requesting that folks see the psychological abuser in a complete picture. They are not a jigsaw puzzle with many pieces that we can pull apart and only look at one piece at a time. Survivors must assemble the entire puzzle and stand back to take in the true picture.

*Many times people find online memes, pictures, or quotes that serve as centerpieces for the truth. These items bring the survivor back to their authentic feelings of disgust with the abuser. That energy pushes them forward to do what must be done to get healthier.*

One way survivors can help themselves while in the *Despair* stage is by not minimizing their anger. Frequently, survivors will attempt to push aside their feelings of irritation, anger, or even rage. Why do they do this? Because the belief is that nice people don't let their anger overcome them. Is out of control anger wise? Not at all and it can lead to even more issues. Allowing the anger to arise—because of the way their lives have been affected by abusers—should serve as a driving force of change. In order to stay connected to their feelings that serve as a motivation towards personal growth, sometimes survivors need visual reminders of what they have lived through. Example? Many times people find online memes, pictures, or quotes that serve as centerpieces for the truth. These items bring the survivor back to their authentic feelings of disgust with the abuser. That energy pushes them forward to do what must be done to get healthier. We cannot heal if we fail to stay in reality. Fantasies of what might be, what could have been, or what should have been are very counterproductive to recovery. The truths that are hard to look at are the exact things a weary soul must see in order to be driven to change current life situations.

# STAGE TWO: EDUCATION

*Psychological abuse is exceptionally insidious and there-fore misunderstood. That is precisely part of the abuser(s) tactic to keep the abuse hidden and remain firmly in control. A victim cannot begin recovery if they can't describe what has been done to them. Learning the common methods employed by psychological abusers is Stage Two. Survivors new to recovery should know what the following terms mean in relationship to psychological abuse:*

- *Gaslighting*
- *Smear Campaign*
- *Flying Monkeys*
- *Narcissistic Offense*
- *Intermittent Reinforcement*
- *Idealize, Devalue, and Discard Phases*

*There are other terms, but for Stage Two, this list is a great starting point for those seeking recovery.*

Gaslighting? Flying Monkeys? I know. Some of the terms associated with this form of abuse sound odd at first. Once we have gone through exactly what they mean, you will definitely see how these words have played out in your own life.

## Gaslighting

What in the world is gaslighting? Great question. Back in the 1940s, there was a movie with a similar title. It followed the story of a husband who set out to make his wife behave and look "crazy." I won't give a spoiler as to why he needed her to be unstable, but suffice it to say he systematically tore apart her world and her confidence in herself. It was done through the brainwashing technique now known as gaslighting.

When an abuser gaslights, he or she sets up situations to make the target doubt their own memories and assessments of situations. This is done in order that survivors will become so unsure of themselves they hand over reign of their lives to the abusers. Surely if the targets are as unreliable as the abusers show them to be, how can they possibly manage themselves? This is exactly the plan. Examples? Absolutely. These examples are fictional to illustrate a point. If they sound like real life situations, it's only by coincidence:

- In the moment it happens, you try to point out how your partner's specific words are very hurtful. Instead of listening to what you are saying, she or he repeats back only part of what you said to them. You repeat yourself, and again he or she replies with only a portion of the conversation. As you continue in this spin cycle, you move further away from the original issues. Eventually your partner sternly says something like, "If you can't even be trusted to remember your own words, how can we have good communication?!" You apologize because it is true. You got lost in the conversation and your partner did not. Something must be wrong with you.

- You know you left an important work file on your desk, with plans to take it to a meeting later in the day. When you go to grab it, you realize the file is gone. You search your entire desk and begin looking in other areas of the office. As you rush by a toxic co-worker, he or she asks what you're doing, so you explain. The co-worker says, "Oh, I found this in the copy room," and hands you the missing file. You are very confused because you have absolutely no recollection of taking it with you to that room. Your co-worker sees your confused look and says something like, "Good thing I am here to clean up your messes." You thank the co-worker and walk away feeling really dysfunctional. Good grief. You can't even keep track of important files.

- Your toxic mother-in-law (TMIL) likes to remind you of all your husband's ex-girlfriends and how close they were to the family. One ex still comes over for dinner and stays the night at the family home as she is considered "another daughter." Your TMIL makes no effort to hide that she is devastated this ex-girlfriend was not her son's choice for a wife. There is palpable tension between you and your TMIL. Her continuous mention of the ex-girlfriend rubs you wrong, but you try to rise above it. You remind yourself that your husband picked you, not the other woman, to marry. While getting ready to go out to a spur-of-the-moment event with your in-laws and husband, you realize you are not dressed for the occasion. Don't worry. Your TMIL has an immediate solution. She goes to the closet in the guest bedroom, pulls out a woman's dress that is probably a little too small for you and slyly says, "You might be able to wear this. It's Tiffany's old dress." (Tiffany, aka beloved ex-girlfriend). You stand there, dumbfounded, that your TMIL keeps the ex's old clothes in the guest room, that she is offering it to you, and your husband thinks nothing wrong of you possibly wearing it. You're super uncomfortable with the whole situation, but they see it as perfectly normal. What's wrong with you? Maybe you really are that insecure and weak. It is just a dress. *A dress that is too small.* The TMIL didn't mean to hurt your feelings, or did she?

- You grew up in a home where you were told that success is the only measure of a person's worth. Success in everything you did was the unspoken requirement. At times, it was even blatantly stated. The clear message was that if you were not successful, it reflected badly on the family. You strived for perfection in every area of your life. One day you earned a very prestigious award at school. You were beyond excited to share the news with your parents, and have them be proud of you. You could hardly wait to tell them about the award, but when you were done excitedly sharing the news they looked at you blankly, and one said, "We didn't raise you to be so arrogant! Do you think you're the only one who has good news today? Why do you think you are more important than other people in this family?!" You didn't mean to be rude. You did look forward to telling them, so maybe you are an arrogant jerk. Look how hard you always work to win stupid awards. Your parents are right. You think way too much of yourself.

- You're on staff at a church. A toxic pastor calls you into his office and tells you to leave the door open. The pastor speaks in a low, stern voice, and he never loses eye contact with you. He proceeds to tell you about the administrative mistake you made. As you attempt to explain why you do not see it as a mistake, he holds his hand up towards your face and says, "Stop making excuses." He leans closer, locks eyes on you and states, "The only correct answer is 'Sorry.'" You mumble the apology and leave the meeting, shaking. You later bring it up to another church leader, but when questioned about the meeting, the toxic pastor emphatically states that the door was left open, that people were sitting right outside the office (which is true), and that you were insubordinate because you did not take his leadership seriously. He accuses you of being rebellious and openly questions your appropriateness for being a member of the church staff.

You spend the rest of the day, and several days after, wondering if you are unfit for ministry.

You can see from these few examples of gaslighting that psychological abuse can be very slippery and slimy. It's called hidden abuse for a reason. Abusers are out for emotional blood when they use gaslighting to under-mine a target's sense of self. They know exactly what they do. They want the survivors to look petty in the eyes of other people. They want them to question themselves and their grasp on reality. They want survivors to fall apart so they can better control or mock them.

*Abusers are out for emotional blood when they use gaslighting to undermine a target's sense of self.*

### Smear Campaign

If psychological abusers cannot get their targets to question themselves—and turn inward to self-loathing—the abusers will surely try to turn the opinions of others against the survivors. Perhaps both tactics will be used. A smear campaign is meant to ei-ther isolate the target so he or she only has the abuser to turn to for "help," or it is meant to prove that the abuser is justified in their treatment of the survivor.

A calculated smear campaign might look something like the following fictional scenarios:

- A co-worker says he dropped an important file on your desk right before a vital meeting, but you can't find it anywhere. You turn your entire desk upside down looking for it. As you nervously walk into the conference room, the toxic co-worker has the file in his hand. When you question him about why he said he left it on your desk, he mockingly tells you he never said that. He darts his eyes towards the important people in the room and makes the face of fake concern about your memory.

- Your toxic mother-in-law (TMIL) asks your child, "Would you like to go to the movies?" Of course, the child excitedly says, "Yes!" and the TMIL goes off to her room to get ready to leave. The TMIL never asked you or your spouse if it was okay for the child to go to the movies. When she comes out of her room ready to leave, you have to tell her and your child that today isn't a good day to go because of other plans that were already made. Now your child is having a disappointment fueled meltdown, and the TMIL stands there fake crying, and whining, "All I wanted to do was have a good day with my grandbaby!"

- Your friend invites you to a party and says it's going to be a very casual pool party. You were told to come in your bathing suit for an evening of fun. You arrive only to see it is a poolside cocktail party, and you're the only schmuck in swim attire. The friend makes a loud sarcastic announcement, "Oh, here comes the one person who can never follow instructions!" Everyone laughs, and you look like the idiot who can't follow instructions, again.

- You're one of four kids. The three other siblings get

together on a regular basis, but never call to include you. When you finally decide to be upfront about your feelings of being isolated, you talk to one of your siblings and find out that years ago your parents told all of your siblings that you did not like them. They were told that you had problems with the siblings' life choices. This couldn't be further from the truth. Even though you try to explain that your mom and dad lied about you, your siblings don't believe your parents would do such a thing and conclude that you are merely blaming two elderly people. This just adds to the discord between you and the other family members because what type of monster attacks their parents by calling them liars? They are and they did.

- You're on staff at a church. A toxic pastor calls you into his office and tells you to leave the door open. The pastor speaks in a low, stern voice, and he never loses eye contact with you. He proceeds to tell you about the administrative mistake you made. As you attempt to explain why you do not see it as a mistake, he holds his hand up towards your face and says, "Stop making excuses." He leans closer, locks eyes on you and states, "The only correct answer is 'Sorry.'" You mumble the apology and leave the meeting, shaking. You later bring it up to another church leader, but when questioned about the meeting, the toxic pastor emphatically states that the door was left open, that people were sitting right outside the office (which is true), and that you were insubordinate because you did not take his leadership seriously. He accuses you of being rebellious and openly questions your appropriateness for being a member of the church staff.

Wait, wasn't this church example used to highlight gaslighting? Yes, indeed. But the difference is that now, under smear campaign, the survivor isn't questioning herself (or himself) because the internal dialog of being fit for ministry has been taken out of this equation. The survivor knows what was said in that meeting and can see the toxic pastor is attempting to turn other people against him or her. It's a subtle difference, but a critically important one.

## Flying Monkeys

The idea of flying monkeys comes from the movie, *The Wizard of Oz* and how the Wicked Witch of the West used her troop of monkeys to fly off and do the evil work for her. Narcissists, sociopaths, and psychopaths have their monkeys too. I have no doubt you have had a run in with these human, winged creatures. Toxic people manipulate two types of helpers to do their dirty work: 1) innocent people who don't see the abuse, and 2) individuals who purposefully ignore the abuse. Toxic people have an incredible ability to triangulate their helpers into abusing survivors. This is done on purpose so the toxic person's hands stay clean from the abuse. It's hard to pin responsibility on an abuser when he or she wasn't even in the same room when the offense took place. However, the use of flying monkeys is like an abuser

*Toxic people have an incredible ability to triangulate their helpers into abusing survivors. This is done on purpose so the toxic person's hands stay clean from the abuse. It's hard to pin responsibility on an abuser when he or she wasn't even in the same room when the offense took place.*

pulling the pin on a grenade and watching from a safe distance as the destruction takes place. The abuser sets it all into motion, but is nowhere to be found on the actual crime scene. Clever. This level of detailed thought just proves an abuser's actions are not random. The abuser must keep all the plates spinning at once and never look like the bad guy or gal. There is no way someone could ever convince me that narcissists, sociopaths, and psychopaths are clueless about their behaviors. The level at which they are able to recruit flying monkeys to the dark side with them is stunning.

Let's first take a look at the flying monkeys who really do not understand they are being used by a psychological abuser. These individuals honestly and truly do not get it. Should they get it? Maybe. Probably. Perhaps they are sticking their heads in the ground so as not to see what is too ugly to take in its full form. I know there are those who condone abuse through silence, and that's our second group of monkeys. In this first section, let's stick with those who don't know about the abuse. An example might be someone who hears the lies about a survivor through a smear campaign. She or he really doesn't know the abuser except by their public persona, which is commonly some form of a servant or good public leader. The unsuspecting flying monkey therefore assumes a misplaced offense on behalf of the abuser. Example? Let's say a survivor is dealing with toxic in-laws. The in-laws like to smear their scapegoat daughter-in-law to all the in-law's church friends. The in-laws may even use crocodile tears to share their sadness about how their son has married a cold hearted woman who has torn their son away from his loving family. Not exactly the truth, but with toxic people the truth is irrelevant to their agenda. These abusive in-laws elicit the sympathies of unsuspecting people who don't really know the in-laws are actually personality disordered and very different people behind the safety of their house walls.

Fast forward to a random grocery store: the son and daughter-in-law are shopping and run into a family friend who knows the son through his parents' church ties. The family friend glares at the daughter-in-law. Then goes into a long story about how wonderful her in-laws are and how they are shining examples of Christian love. The son and daughter-in-law have encountered an unsuspecting flying monkey. The family friend has no idea what the truth is and merely took the words of the toxic in-laws at face value. Should this family friend have taken the time to get to know the daughter-in-law before passing judgment? Absolutely. But this individual didn't and instead based an attitude towards the daughter-in-law solely on the words of people who were believed to be trustworthy. They look like normal people from the outside looking in, so why would an average person think abuse was hidden within the family?

Just like in our grocery store example, this type of flying monkey comes flapping their wings to tell you all about how you need to get along better with your parents, in-laws, supervisor, co- worker, friend, or church leader. This person basically listened to the toxic lies by the abuser, was handed a time-released grenade, walked in your direction, and let the emotional grenade go off when they saw you. They have come to do the bidding of the abuser (aka The Wicked Witch). Flying monkeys in this form do not see the damage they do, do not really get the full picture of the relational issues, and are annoying static noise in the ears of survivors. These flying monkeys are reminders of just how much the abuser wants people to think poorly of the survivor. They also highlight the fact that a psychologically abusive person has no moral compass and is more than willing to use innocent peo-

> *Flying monkeys in this form do not see the damage they do, do not really get the full picture of the relational issues, and are annoying static noise in the ears of survivors.*

ple as pawns to further the horrendous treatment of the scapegoated survivor.

The second type of flying monkey is very aware of the hidden abuse. They see it, like it on some level, and play along by keeping the abuser supplied with encouragement. Insane, I know, but it is the truth nonetheless. This kind of flying monkey can take the form of one of the mean step-sisters to Cinderella, and on behalf of the even meaner step-mom. The sisters play a critical role in normalizing abnormal behaviors, and that is the exact function of this category of flying monkeys. They basically serve as encouragement for the abuser. When the toxic person complains about a target of their abuse, the enabling flying monkeys stoke the flames of gossip and hatred. They even supply more information for the abuser to use against the survivor. When thinking of this second type of flying monkeys, I often picture clusters of dysfunctional family members gathered together talking about a scapegoat individual who isn't present. I also see a small group of co-workers whose hidden plot is to make another employee look incompetent. They are also small groups of peers who say they don't gossip, yet always seem to be talking about the same person each time the group gets together. The well-aware flying monkeys may not be clusters of people, but they can be toxic individuals themselves. Their damage is just as harmful. Validating the abuse through their approval makes them guilty as co-conspirators to psychological abuse.

Flying monkeys can be found everywhere. Wherever there is a psychologically abusive person, at least one flying monkey will be lurking nearby. In the workplace, the toxic person might be a passive-aggressive employee who has run off every team member assigned to work with him or her. This individual has a supervisor who cleans up the mess after every new person implodes while in the role, mirroring the abusive person. Rather than dealing with the toxic staff person, the supervisor goes off to find the next target employee to hand over to the abuser. The issue of going through multiple people because of the toxic team member is never addressed by the flying monkey supervisor. Maybe the supervisor and the abusive person get along outside of work, perhaps they have known each other for years, or the supervisor is playing out some people-pleasing dance with the toxic person. Whatever the reason toxic behaviors are tolerated in a company, the bottom line is that it takes flying monkeys to cover up chronic bad behaviors by an abuser.

Religious organizations are notorious for the clustering of flying monkeys around an abusive person. All in the name of God, hidden abuse is shoved down even further. It is buried under a mound of lies and done so to protect the projection of a perfect religious image. I have witnessed some of the worst forms of flying monkeys while observing toxic churches and their leaders. Not only are people made into flying monkeys to support the gaslighting and smear campaigns against targets, guess who else is developed into a flying monkey? God. God of the Bible is the culture with which I am most familiar, and I can share with you without hesitation, psychological abusers are using God as a flying monkey. They do this by hurling accusations at the survivor about what God would want, what God thinks, and what God says about the survivor's attitude towards

*Not only are people made into flying monkeys to support the gaslighting and smear campaigns against targets, guess who else is developed into a flying monkey? God.*

the toxic leader. Abusive church leadership must minimize God to a puppet that can be moved around at will, and it smells of blasphemy to me. It is most noticeable in denominations on either extreme of the legalistic or charismatic scale. Two sides of the teeter-totter. This is because in the legalistic church, God (or pronounced "Gawd" if you're in the southern regions of the country) is coming to smite those individuals who dare defy His earthly leadership. How dare you, survivor, try to bring any abuse to light? There are rules to be followed and questioning leadership, especially male leadership, is not to be tolerated. On the other seat of the playground teeter-totter are the charismatic environments that breed the ability for narcissistic, sociopathic, or psychopathic religious leaders to say God told them this or that about a survivor. God told the toxic leader that the survivor is "not walking right with God" or has a "Jezebel spirit," or any number of other spirits the abusive leader chooses to use against whomever they target for abuse. It is nearly impossible to openly question a religious leader who starts a conversation with, "God told me..." What recourse does a survivor have beyond, "Well, God didn't tell me the same thing." Can you guess what happens next? The leader clearly is the one to be believed as an authority of being able to hear God because, after all, look at the position of power and influence God has given to him or her. When God becomes a flying monkey to a poisonous religious leader, a vicious mingling of psychological abuse and spiritual abuse congeal.

*When God becomes a flying monkey to a poisonous religious leader, a vicious mingling of psychological abuse and spiritual abuse congeal.*

The ability of narcissists, sociopaths, and psychopaths to make flying monkeys out of a number of people should not be taken lightly. They even have an ability to manipulate counseling sessions and some therapists. Yes, therapists can become flying monkeys. Some know they are being used by toxic people. Since the therapists are toxic themselves, it works in favor of the abusers to further harm survivors. Aligning with the abuser against the target brings some level of entertainment for a toxic therapist. I believe this is rare, but I know this type of triangulation does occur. The vast majority of therapists who become flying monkeys, or tools for the abuser to utilize, are therapists who don't realize what they have encountered. The level of manipulation they are dealing with from the unrecognized psychological abuse blinds them to being valuable as therapists. There are many trained mental health professionals who struggle to initially recognize insidious relational abuse. As a therapist, it is hard at times to sort through the issues a couple or family presents. We even have the education and discernment to help us. At the beginning of therapy, it is a challenge. Becoming a flying monkey to an abuser is a risk if therapists are not keenly aware of the signs and symptoms of hidden abuse.

### Narcissistic Offense (aka Toxic Person Offense)

Narcissistic Offense is when narcissists, sociopaths, and psychopaths take a wrong done to them and blow it completely out of proportion. Do not let the title of Narcissistic Offense confuse you that this term applies only to narcissists. It does not. Personality disordered individuals have over-inflated egos that cannot handle even the smallest of bruising. It is often argued that they are easily offended because they are insecure. They are not insecure. I understand why some people come to the conclusion that the behaviors the toxic person exhibits can *look* like they are covering up an insecurity or a fragile ego, but from a therapeutic perspective, it is not insecurity at all. It is exceptionally dangerous when survivors see abuse through the lens of the abuser being broken or wounded (i.e., insecure). It has a way of completely watering down the truth that abusers know exactly what they do; they make a freewill choice to continue in their harmful ways. Some even get energy—or entertainment—out of jacking around with other people's well-being. As sick as it sounds, it is still the truth.

Narcissistic Offense (aka Toxic Person Offense) explains why they are not insecure. They don't want any flaws or faults pointed out to them. Some people will argue narcissists, sociopaths, and psychopaths overcompensate by trying to dominate and control others in an attempt to deal with their insecurities. Realizing toxic people are not actually insecure is one of the hardest concepts for survivors because thinking toxic people struggle with insecurities is a form of justification for their bad behaviors. We may not want to admit it, but we soften when we think of someone struggling with self-doubt. It is just human nature. Rather than being insecure, psychological abusers are easily offended, consumed with

*Realizing toxic people are not actually insecure is one of the hardest concepts for survivors because thinking toxic people struggle with insecurities is a form of justification for their bad behaviors.*

themselves, and want things just their way.

Each one of us receives evidence every day that we are not perfect. We laugh at ourselves and go on with our lives. Personality disordered people (narcissists, sociopaths, and psychopaths) do not. They work hard to show no vulnerabilities that would indicate flaws because they don't believe they have any flaws. They might cry or say they know they are broken people, but wait for that fleeting moment to end, and they are right back to their arrogant baseline selves. The efforts to cover up their humanness are often misunderstood as insecurity. The motivation underneath their behaviors is what is typically confusing. It is not self-doubt, by definition of the disorders. If you look at the diagnostic criteria for Narcissistic Personality Disorder or Anti-Social Personality Disorder, nowhere is there an indication they will struggle with a true lack of confidence. Words like "grandiose" are included in the diagnoses. Some are covert (hidden) in their grandiosity, but it's still there lurking underneath the façade. Toxic people absolutely refuse to have normal human flaws and weaknesses. They do not see themselves as average people. Their attempts to remove themselves from making mistakes look like a weak ego. It is the fact of life showing them they are not perfect that has collided with their self-image. Therefore, they rage against it.

Narcissistic Offense happens when survivors attempt to show toxic people the mistakes they made, or talk about an obvious need for growth in an area of their lives. Rather than taking the comments as they were intended, psychological abusers will either lash out or give the silent treatment. Perhaps even a combination of a few different forms of punishment will be utilized. This over-exaggeration often leaves survivors dumbfounded, and initially they blame themselves for not choosing their words more carefully. The truth is there is no right way to deliver a correction, or talk about dissatisfaction with narcissists, sociopaths, or psychopaths. They will not take any concerns seriously, and will in fact turn the situation around on survivors. It becomes the survivor's fault for being so rude, disrespectful, and for upsetting them. Personality disordered people do not take too favorably to having their faults pointed out, regardless of how gently the topic is broached.

## Intermittent Reinforcement

Yes, we enter the lovely world of human conditioning. Intermittent reinforcement is basically how people are brainwashed. B.F. Skinner developed a term called "operant conditioning." This sort of conditioning trains survivors to anxiously anticipate when abusers will intermittently reinforce the connection between the two individuals. There is no rhyme or reason to their level of attention or affection. Sometimes it is based on the survivor playing by the abuser's rules. Other times abusers do not respond the way that would have been expected. There is no set pattern for survivors to learn in order to try and stay out of trouble with the abuser. I know, it's a little complicated. Let me give an example:

*Boy likes girl. Girl acts like she likes boy, but she appears to be a narcissist (maybe even a sociopath), so her typical responses to boy are irrational at best. Boy works hard to not do the things that girl has clearly shown him she doesn't like (as evidenced by her screaming, yelling, and name calling). Boy makes a mistake and girl responds lovingly. Boy is deeply confused because he expected her wrath. Boy tries to do something nice for girl and she flips out on him. Boy is even more confused. Girl abruptly disappears for two weeks and has no communication with boy, even though he is "blowing up" her phone trying to figure out where she is and what happened to their relationship. Boy is still in despair when girl pops back up and is sugary sweet. She tells boy she was just super busy and didn't mean to ignore him. Boy is incredibly relieved his life is back to normal.*

Now, repeat this entire paragraph dozens of times, and you have a working example of intermittent reinforcement. The boy is left confused, walking on egg shells, and tightly hanging on to the roller coaster seat as it twists and turns on the girl's ever-changing moods. The most important point is that the girl's moods are not changing because she's moody. She is conditioning the boy to always be off balance. Off balance. Some toxic people will actually say out loud that they like keeping people off balance. If someone tells you that, run. It is a huge red flag that you are talking to a psychological manipulator. The boy in my vignette clings to the idea that things will get better, and that the girl will stop acting so bizarrely because she does have really great days too. The problem with hoping for a miracle is that the hope is not based in reality. Toxic people cannot sustain any length of relationship connection (i.e., the good days). As mentioned

> *Toxic people cannot sustain any length of relationship connection (i.e., the good days). As mentioned before, their lack of healthy attachments while growing up, and their refusal to deal with their flaws, creates the perfect storm for their inability to have stable relationships.*

before, their lack of healthy attachments while growing up, and their refusal to deal with their flaws, creates the perfect storm for their inability to have stable relationships. Most will even admit the idea of a normal relationship is boring to them. They thrive on the mental games and chaos that always follows them around. If they are not entertained by turmoil, they will at least be more comfortable with little or no authentic attachments in their relationships.

Intermittent reinforcement also takes place in a work setting, family, or church. The concepts of never knowing what to expect, and feeling relief when the abuser is pleased, can both serve as signals that you might be intermittently reinforced to stay dancing with an abuser. I saw a post online where someone said, "An abuser doesn't abuse every day." That, my friend, is intermittent reinforcement in a nutshell. The problem is a survivor never knows when the next warm and fuzzy experience will happen, or when the next episode of abuse is coming through the door. Intermittent reinforcement is a powerful emotional string abusers like to pull. Never knowing what will happen next can be intoxicating for a survivor who is not fully aware of the game being played. Intermittent reinforcement causes adrenaline rushes in the body and stress hormones to be produced. It creates a biochemical shift in the survivor that becomes addicting and from which is hard to break free. Detoxing from an unhealthy bond is possible, and we will cover that more in *Stage Four: Boundaries.*

## Idealize, Devalue, & Discard Phases

We have now arrived at the backbone of the life cycle for psychologically abusive relationships. Again, it isn't limited to romantic relationships. These three phases are applicable in different environments.

### Idealize

The *Idealize* phase is when manipulators and their new targets first meet. You were once the new target. In this phase, abusers are sizing you up, listening, and learning everything they can about you. This is done so they can mirror back someone who would be the perfect romantic partner, co-worker, or friend. It is during this phase that any survivor feels incredibly lucky to have found someone so wonderful to be his or her mentor, best friend, or even soul mate. Abusers are very careful not to mirror too much or overplay their hand to make the game obvious. They show just enough differences not to set off any warnings about their trickery. Sadly, that is exactly what happened. You were fully being yourself and the abuser was a chameleon. The abuser morphed to fit your ideal role.

Within the realm of romantic relationships, terms like love bombing are applicable at this phase. Love bombing occurs when a toxic person floods the target's world with expressions of love. It is often done quickly in the relationship, and in a manner that amplifies the body chemistry (e.g., oxytocin and dopamine). These biochemical changes in the target are normal when someone is falling in love. The grave problem with hidden abuse is the target is being manipulated. The feelings are being manufactured for the power and control of an abuser, but the target doesn't know it yet. The target thinks she or he has met someone wonderful, possibly even "the one."

In the setting of work or church, this *Idealize* phase might look like someone acting as if she or he wants to be a mentor to a target. The abuser may work fast and furiously to get the target on board to quickly share intimate details about himself or herself. This is done to create a dependency on the connection and allow the abuser to gain unguarded access to the target's hopes, dreams, failings, and goals. Later on, these same personal treasures can be exploited for the abuser's gain or just for plain entertainment. It is very hard to conceive that people actually get enjoyment out of this sick game, but they do. We must come to terms with that fact so that healing can begin.

### Devalue

The next phase occurs after the target is fully hooked. The dependency is created, and the survivor feels on top of the world because of her or his new connection. Now comes the hard fall from the pedestal—a huge human splat onto the concrete floor. This

*The grave problem with hidden abuse is the target is being manipulated. The feelings are being manufactured for the power and control of an abuser, but the target doesn't know it yet. The target thinks she or he has met someone wonderful, possibly even "the one."*

phase is incredibly emotionally messy. The *Devalue* phase is when the survivor's world starts to suddenly implode. Remember all that love bombing and extra attention that was present earlier? Those exact compliments and attention now become all the rocks that are thrown at the target. Stone by stone. Bruise by bruise. The survivor's perfect romantic interest, mentor, or friend has abruptly turned on her or him. It's a crushing season in life. How could someone who once professed love, or deep respect, now be the exact same person who is stealthily abusive? Welcome to the vile world of personality disordered people.

Narcissists, sociopaths, and psychopaths are notorious for picking targets who initially boost their egos. It could be the target's appearance, age, intellect, career success, family, friends, or so on. Once the target is hooked during the previous *Idealize* phase, the toxic person sets out to tear down the exact qualities that attracted him or her to the survivor in the first place. This is now the *Devalue* phase and all the misery that comes with it. As I mentioned before, toxic people do not pick weak people as their targets. This is a common misconception among survivors. On the contrary, psychologically abusive people set out to take down the biggest challenge that presented itself at the time. The abuser sees it as a huge victory to turn an independent survivor into a needy, dependent person who can no longer make

> *The abuser sees it as a huge victory to turn an independent survivor into a needy, dependent person who can no longer make decisions without the abusive person's help.*

decisions without the abusive person's help. The abuser often complains about how weak the survivor has become, but it is exactly the abuser's actions that have made the changes. Blaming the survivor is the ultimate insult. Many targets experience deep levels of shame when they realize how different they have become while in these relationships.

Quite a few people stay right here in the *Devalue* phase with the abuser. They are rooted in what the *Idealize* phase felt like and these survivors try desperately to get back to those magical days of feeling important. Those days will never return because it was only the bait on the hook in order to catch them. There is no real substance that can be resurrected later on in these relationships. Some people wonder if abusers can feel love or affection for their targets. The answer to that depends on your own definition of love. Abusers can have fleeting moments of acting like they care about others, because in those moments, the loving actions serve the abusers in some way. Survivors must remember that every interaction is always about the abuser and their own needs. Any expressions of passion or appreciation given by toxic people are somehow to their benefit. If your definition of love is wanting to see another person authentically happy and living a fulfilled life, then the answer is no. Psychological abusers cannot feel love. They can only mimic what love looks like. Some do a good job of acting, but only for a calculated season.

## Discard

The target was acquired (*Idealize* phase), the target was emotionally harmed (*Devalue* phase), and now we begin the grand finale of rejecting the target (*Discard* phase). The reason this last phase differs vastly from other relationship endings is because a survivor is left—not only with the loss of connection—but their entire personhood has been shredded as well. A survivor's body is often in need of physical healing because of the psychological abuse. Their self-image has been altered. Often times there are huge lifestyle losses that have come along while in the abuse. By the time the *Discard* phase occurs, a survivor's world is unsafe and in upheaval. Again, there is a spectrum of abusive behaviors and a spectrum of survivor responses. For the majority of survivors, encounters with psychological abusers have a life-altering result. The level of impact on a target's life will also be different depending on whether the abuse took place in a marriage or relationship, at work, among peers, in

*The level of impact on a target's life will also be different depending on whether the abuse took place in a marriage or relationship, at work, among peers, in a family, or at church. The closer the abuser is to the center of a survivor's daily life, the more damage that can be perpetrated.*

a family, or at church. The closer the abuser is to the center of a survivor's daily life, the more damage that can be perpetrated.

The discard by the psychological abuser is often very evil and shaming. I have heard all sorts of different stories about how discards can take place, and they leave me grieving for the survivors. If you have been discarded by an abuser, I am sure you have your own set of battle scars. Road rash from having been tossed from a moving relationship vehicle. Perhaps you were the one to end the relationship. Believe me when I say that I know you did not escape easily. By the time survivors are compelled to leave their psychologically abusive relationships, they do not see any other viable option but to leave. They have tried anything and everything to keep their relationship going. No matter how hard they tried to fit the mold the abuser wanted, it was never enough. Never good enough, and always somehow wrong.

Remember that research project Dr. John and I conducted on patterns of psychological abuse? One of the questions asked about what made a survivor go No Contact. I am going to discuss this topic later in the next chapter on *Boundaries*, but for now, I want to share with you that 298 participants wrote in answers to the question, "Please provide specific examples of what the breaking point was when you went "No Contact" with the abusive person." (No Contact is when a victim no longer participates in contact of any form with the perpetrator). Of the 298 responses, the most common themes were the survivor leaving the relationship because of extreme acts of violence by the abuser. Survivors being seriously threatened or actually harmed were the main reasons for a target to finally end the relationship. Very few responses did not involve some sort of big finale blow up. This level of catastrophe is needed to finally break it off because by the time the *Discard* phase occurs, the survivor has been so thoroughly programmed to stay with the abuser.

As you can see, the *Idealize*, *Devalue*, and *Discard* phases are foundational to understanding the course of psychologically abusive relationships. Survivors often wonder how these three phases are any different than the normal phases for all relationships. It's a legitimate question. How does the story go?

*Two people meet. They are attracted to one another. They start spending oodles of time together. There are lots of love notes, gifts, and endless hours on the phone together. They can't get one another out of their thoughts. Time goes by, and their differences start to show. They don't see eye-to-eye on the things they thought they once did. Arguments become more frequent, but they are each trying to dust themselves off and keep going forward in the relationship. Eventually, one or both realize it isn't working and a break-up occurs. They may meet afterwards to talk about the relationship and to get closure, but ultimately, the connection died and a lifelong relationship is not to be.*

The difference between that scenario of a normal dating pattern and the break-up of a psychologically abusive relationship lies squarely in the motivation behind the behaviors. In a normal situation, both people want to meet the one they can be with for the rest of their lives. Both people are starting out the relationship with honesty and authenticity to make the relationship work. Both people are capable of forming healthy relationship attachments. When a psychologically abusive relationship starts, only the target is feeling normal connections. The abuser is just there to feed some sense of power and to fill up time in his or her daily life. Two completely different situations; one is normal and one is abusive.

As we conclude our time in *Stage Two: Education*, I want you to know there are many words used in the psychological abuse recovery community that are helpful to understanding the abuse and the healing process. I personally think these eight terms are a perfect place to start. As your journey through recovery continues, you will find more that resonate with you. For now, congratulations for reading through the first two stages of recovery. Our next stop? *Awakening*.

# STAGE THREE: AWAKENING

*When survivors have identified their Despair from hav-*
*ing been psychologically abused (Stage One), and then*
*Educated themselves on the specific ways abusers harm*
*others (Stage Two), an Awakening happens for the sur-*
*vivor (Stage Three). This is the point in recovery when*
*many aha moments happen. Survivors can describe what*
*they experienced, have learned new terminology, and in*
*doing so, no longer feel isolated in the abuse. At this stage,*
*a survivor may start to feel empowered in their recovery*
*journey. However, there are good days and bad days. It is*
*common for survivors to swing back to Despair and then*
*forward to Awakening again. This is normal and part of*
*the process of deprogramming and healing from the psy-*
*chological abuse.*

This is also the stage where anger may really arrive
onto the scene. People often say that this stage of awakening brings out a level of feistiness survivors have not
previously experienced. They say things like:

"I can believe evil is real in the world. I have seen it."

"What I have lived through actually has a name, and other people know what I have experienced."

"That troll had me convinced I was the problem!"

"Turns out, I am not bat-crazy after all."

"I can't believe they have done this to me."

See the theme? It's all good. Sometimes we need to just speak and not worry about filtering our words. Recovery from psychological abuse involves having the freedom to be our authentic selves, not some watered down versions so as not to offend the delicate senses of finicky abusers. You know what? Be yourself. That is what this *Awakening* stage is dedicated to doing. It is a stage of coming to terms with the, "How dare they treat me like this?" question. It's an awakening, but not some soft, delicate rebirthing like a butterfly out of a cocoon awakening. It is a tearing down walls awakening. At times, it is an angry awakening. It is definitely bittersweet. Becoming fully aware of the dynamics of psychological abuse is not an easy truth to absorb. It is necessary to see but exceptionally disappointing and painful at the same time. The frenzied spinning stops at this stage, but the deprogramming has not yet fully happened.

*Becoming fully aware of the dynamics of psychological abuse is not an easy truth to absorb.*

This *Awakening* stage involves spurts of awareness followed by *Despair* again. It includes moments and glimmers of clarity to show survivors they really are dealing with a hidden bona fide snake in human form. The awakening feeling—or sense of clarity—is hard to hold on to at this stage of recovery. It is like fists full of sand that slips through the finger cracks. One minute survivors feel a sense of empowerment, and the next they sob because they miss the abuser. Everything in them wants to believe the abuser can change. Some people try to hold on to the excuse that toxic people had bad childhoods or some other trauma that makes them behave the way they do. Deep down survivors know they are making excuses for poor behaviors. Facing the truth about those we have loved (e.g., our parents, siblings, a treasured friend, or a spiritual leader) is unbelievably hard, but there is no glory in clinging to a lie because the truth is too painful to accept.

One of the excuses survivors of abuse try to make is that maybe toxic people have an underlying mental illness. It could be true, but my experience as a therapist is most people who are personality disordered do not have other mental health issues driving their noxious behaviors. I can say that not everyone who exhibits sporadic mood swings is a narcissist, sociopath, or psychopath. Untreated Bipolar Disorder is one diagnosis that comes to mind when thinking about erratic behavior. There are other personality disorders (such as Borderline Personality Disorder) and they do not have the exact same features as Narcissistic Personality Disorder or

Anti-Social Personality Disorder. Post-Traumatic Stress Disorder (PTSD) can often mimic some of the pushing away of people and turmoil producing behaviors we see in narcissists, sociopaths, and psychopaths. However, Bipolar Disorder, Borderline Personality Disorder, and PTSD stem from vastly diverse causes. The folks dealing with other mental health challenges have very different internal motivations than psychologically abusive narcissists, sociopaths, and psychopaths. The one really important component to remember is these toxic people lack empathy. People who are diagnosed as having Bipolar Disorder, PTSD, or even Borderline Personality Disorder still have an ability to see how their actions can cause other people harm. They have the capability to feel empathy and authentic care for others. Narcissists, sociopaths, and psychopaths choose to maintain no attachments with those around them. Therefore, should not be trusted with any survivor's mind, body, or soul.

Being able to describe what they have endured is exceptionally powerful for survivors. In the *Despair* stage, that wasn't possible. Having language to describe how they were harmed allows survivors the ability to communicate their pain and newfound healing. As a therapist, I can see the huge difference education makes with clients. We have a common set of words that allow us to communicate more clearly. In doing so, the aha moments start to rise to the surface. A common theme during this *Awakening* stage is disbelief, tempered with a new sense of peace that they are not as broken as the abuser tried to make them believe. During *Stage Three: Awakening*, many survivors sit on the counseling couch in moments of silence. They are just taking in all they have figured out. There are deep breaths of calming air that survivors enjoy. No longer are they an unknowing puppet with strings attached to them. Another image I often use is that of EKG (electro-cardiogram) electrodes. Psychological abusers want to have as many open doors or portals in which to shock and scare the targets. During the *Awakening* stage of recovery, survivors start to symbolically pull off each of the electrodes that have been stuck to them. This is done so toxic people cannot have a direct line to their body or soul. At this point in recovery, nothing may have actually outwardly changed yet in the relationship with the abuser. However, things have dramatically shifted inside the survivor. It is sometimes obvious on their faces. This is the stage when survivors start looking a little more settled and have some strength returning to their speaking voices. Those who were being squashed by the psychological mind games are lifting those burdens off of themselves and starting to stand on their feet again. Their heads are looking up, away from the ground, and making eye contact with others.

Psychological abusers slowly and methodically gain control over their targets. One of the first indicators of abuse is when a target no longer feels they can make independent decisions. As a survivor breaks away and begins to heal from the abuse, she or he will have moments of realizing just how controlled they are, or once were. These moments of clarity often come through everyday decisions, like what to wear, what to eat, or what to buy. While in recovery, having the freedom to make these basic decisions—without fear of criticism—helps the survivor to clearly see the level of control that occurred. These can be complicated moments. Survivors help their own recovery when they can celebrate their growth and not allow shame to overcome them.

After going through *Stage Two: Education*, there is a strong sense of unity with other survivors. For the first time, people realize they are not alone in the hidden crazy-making experiences they have encountered. There are a few books that are tangibly helpful to learning about psychological abuse. I have a very short list of books I recommend. Those names are in the back, in the *Resources* section. As I began my own journey as a therapist to better understand the world of psychological abuse recovery, I was exceptionally stunned to learn of the subculture of online peer support. Every platform of social media is rich with resources offering memes, blog posts, forum discussion boards, online radio shows, secret groups for privacy, and video channels full of education for survivors. As a

> *For the first time, people realize they are not alone in the hidden crazy-making experiences they have encountered.*

newcomer into this world of online support, the collective warmth and open arms were surprising to me. As one advocate said, "After psychological abuse, it's hard to know who to trust, but you can usually trust another survivor." The online friendships that have been made run deep in authenticity. I know many people who have made lifelong connections with others who have lived through the same hidden abuse. Some of the people in my *Acknowledgments* section are folks with whom I have never been in the same room, but they have been a part of my journey specializing in the recovery of psychological abuse. This book would not have happened without the support of individuals whom I have never met in person but have become connected with through social media. They welcomed me into their circle of advocates for survivors, and I am forever grateful. The same level of community is available for you. If you have not ventured into the world of recovery online, I would encourage you to do so. Listed in the *Resources* section are groups and forums I recommend.

One word of caution: when you are online, look for groups and discussions that fit your sense of recovery. There are individuals commonly known as "trolls" and they like to stir up trouble. They are most likely not survivors but actually toxic people anonymously going into groups to be annoying; as if they weren't already annoying enough in person. The groups I have listed in the back work very hard to identify the trolls and boot them off quickly so survivors are not triggered by their words and attitudes.

When the *Awakening* stage happens, getting support is vitally important. These are not terms and concepts you want rattling around alone in your head. Currently, the support options for recovery specific to psychological abuse are in-person therapy and the online peer support I mentioned. My intent in writing this book is to add in-person support groups to the options available to survivors. I think there is power in finding other people who "get it" and who do so on a personal level. The anonymity of online support is very useful to some folks. They are able to use aliases and ask the really hard questions we might be too embarrassed to talk about in person. I know some will benefit greatly from finding safe people after abuse, and in-person book study groups might be just the right venue. The cryptic nature of hidden abuse lends itself to survivors being isolated, and in-person groups will give individuals more options for their recovery process. Sometimes we need to see a warm smile and find a safe place in the real world. We just cannot accomplish that online.

# STAGE FOUR: BOUNDARIES

*After a survivor of psychological abuse has identified their Despair (Stage One), Educated themselves on the specifics of psychological abuse (Stage Two), and had an Awakening that recovery is possible (Stage Three), the next stage is implementing Boundaries. This is the time when survivors choose to implement Detached Contact or No Contact. The important part of this stage is that a survivor is able to gain enough emotional distance to detox from the trauma bonding and start looking forward to their life of recovery. Boundaries are individually driven and must be done in a way that will be followed through on by the survivor. At times, survivors waiver on setting limits with their abuser(s). To set healthy limits may mean the end of the relationship. It is not uncommon for some survivors to get stuck at this stage.*

This is the stage where I wish all survivors could benefit from in-person counseling with a therapist who "gets it." The reason for this desire is because each and every survivor's situation is unique. The subtle nuances

*The subtle nuances of life situations require an individualized plan for boundaries. There is not one blanket statement that covers every single survivor in the entire world.*

of life situations require an individualized plan for boundaries. There is not one blanket statement that covers every single survivor in the entire world. It's a bit grandiose to think we know what is best for everyone else out there roaming the earth. Boundaries need to be implemented so healing can occur. That is the bottom line. How that healing happens is individual. I know some advocates in the psychological abuse recovery community have a staunch No Contact policy. I fully get that stance. As a licensed therapist, I do not have the ethical luxury of insisting clients do what I think is best for them. One of our main guidelines as therapists is to not impose our will or biases on our clients. They get to decide what works in their lives. Am I always painfully honest about the realities of life with a toxic person? Absolutely. I do not cut corners or mince words when working with a client. I often joke I am not a soft and squishy therapist who is going to nod and say, "Tell me more about that." With a passive voice, I would be bored out of my mind counseling each and every day. I attract the clients who desire direct and upfront dialogue. I always say that if my therapeutic approach is not a good fit, I could throw a rock and probably hit several other great therapists within a small radius of my office. My staff and interns often hear me say that there is a therapist for every client, and we don't have to work with everyone who calls our office. We have a duty to help potential clients find the right therapeutic relationship for their recovery to occur because when philosophical differences happen, it brings counseling growth to a screeching halt.

All that to say: I cannot take a blanket No Contact position and remain an ethical therapist. Boundaries must be developed on an individual basis. Effective counseling can help sort through the competing factors that push and pull on a survivor's decision-making abilities. What might be right for a survivor, might not be right for their kids. What might be right for their kids, might not be right for the survivor. What might be right for the survivor's career trajectory, might not be right for the survivor's well-being. This back and forth can be played out with any number of relationships. One I often see? What is right for the survivor's spiritual growth, might not be right for keeping the status quo of her or his church leadership and reputation.

The real challenge with remaining in contact occurs when a survivor has regular encounters with what I will call a low-level narcissist. This person would fit the diagnostic criteria for Narcissistic Personality Disorder—and left unchallenged—would most definitely get worse with age and successful power grabbing. However, I have witnessed these less toxic narcissists respond to firm, clear boundaries set by survivors who are seriously not going to put up with any more nonsense. If you immediately disagree, just hang in there and let me talk this out with you. I have watched survivors come in for counseling who, perhaps under the umbrella of being "good Christians," never felt comfortable speaking up or making their boundaries known. Through counseling, we were able to help them find their calm, yet firm voice. It usually came when they had reached the "I cannot do this anymore" point and were willing to walk away from their relationship if things didn't change. When they started setting limits, it came from a place of power and knowing they were not going to live the way they had been. It might be with a spouse, boss, family member, friend, or a religious leader. The survivor reached her or his "No more" point, and the toxic person recognized the power shift.

After the change in a survivor, I have witnessed times when the toxic person slightly backed down or tried to play nice. These behavioral changes happened because there was something positive to be gained for the abuser. Example? A toxic boss who has a survivor setting limits may go along with some changes because the survivor is a valuable employee who makes the boss look good. A spouse who has tried to exert control might back down when challenged if he or she ultimately is comfortable with the marriage and doesn't want to start over as a single person. Maybe the toxic spouse has a financial reason for keeping the marriage going. A psychologically abusive parent may reluctantly follow boundaries set by an adult child because the parent does not want to be cut off from contact with their grandkids. Whatever the reason an abusive person decides to throttle it back a bit, it is up to the survivor alone to decide what a healthy enough environment looks like for their lives. Do some abusers check themselves in order to keep their own lives comfortable? Yes, they do. Do all abusers care if a survivor gets to a "No more" point? Not at all. Actually, most abusers could care less, and any exertion of empowerment by a survivor will be met with a full-on attack. I want advocates and survivors in the abuse recovery community to recognize that one size does not fit all when it comes to healing.

*I want advocates and survivors in the abuse recovery community to recognize that one size does not fit all when it comes to healing.*

Let's now return to the spectrum of toxic people. On the low end are the clinically diagnosable narcissists who will manage their outward expressions of toxicity when it serves their interests. On the high end are the sociopaths and psychopaths who have no qualms about completely destroying people's lives. In the cases of high level narcissists who border on sociopathy or psychopathy, survivors must really weigh their options regarding the detriment that being in contact will have on their well-being. I have been known to tell survivors, who are remaining in contact with intensely toxic people, that I cannot continue to work with them unless they implement and follow the No Contact rule. Isn't that a contradiction of what I said earlier? Not at all. I said that I cannot ethically say every survivor should go No Contact. I did not say I would enter into therapeutic relationships with those who are killing themselves with their drug of choice, which happens to be a psychological abuser. It would be like having a client sit on the couch across from me with a lethal amount of heroin in a needle jabbed in her or his arm. Am I really expected to just sit there while she or he mainlines the drug and try to talk to them about boundaries? Not going to happen. When survivors get to the point where the relationships are slowly killing them, we must talk about why they won't choose their own lives over pleasing the abusers. Those are the most extreme situations. When they do occur, No Contact is the only option for a life of recovery.

One of the most helpful ways for survivors to determine the full influence toxic people are having on their lives is to view it through the lens of what I call the Balanced Life model. In my office file cabinet, I have a handy-dandy pie chart that is printed and ready to be completed with clients. The Balanced Life pie chart has seven areas that are needed to stay out of the work-home-work-home rut of life. A balanced life will consist of:

- Work/Volunteer/School
- Physical Health
- Spiritual Growth

- Friendships
- Romantic Relationship
- Parenting (if applicable)
- Hobbies

A good journaling exercise is to write down the question, "How does my contact with (fill in the toxic person's name) affect my..." and then work down the list. As a made-up example:

- *How does my contact with Sue (or Bob) affect my work?*
- *How does my contact with Sue (or Bob) affect my physical health?*
- *How does my contact with Sue (or Bob) affect my spiritual growth?*

You get the point. Keep going and journal each of the seven slices of the Balanced Life pie.

Another way of doing this exercise is to write out something like:

- *How does staying in my marriage (or staying in my job) affect my work?*
- *How does staying in my marriage (or staying in my job) affect my physical heath?*
- *How does staying in my marriage (or staying in my job) affect my parenting?*

And so on through the seven areas.

The idea of the exercise is to clearly show survivors how having social contact with an abuser, remaining in a toxic workplace or abusive church environment, is impacting the other areas of their lives. At times,

*When we decide that boundaries are needed, they can be hard to set —and main- tain—if we doubt our- selves and our assessment of the situation. Survivors often wonder if they are overreacting or being too sensitive.*

survivors who have complet- ed this exercise have been sur- prised to see their abusive situa- tions are having limited impact on their entire lives. The other side of that coin is when staying in a lethal situation is destroying multi- ple areas of their lives.

When we decide that boundar- ies are needed, they can be hard to set—and maintain—if we doubt ourselves and our assessment of the situation. Survivors often wonder if they are overreacting or being too sensitive. Psychological abusers love to heave those accusa- tions, so it is hard not to fall into the trap of internalizing their words as truth. We need to set healthy boundaries if the behaviors of oth- ers show their lack of respect for us and our health. Boundaries do not have to be melodra- matic or forceful in their application. Boundaries can be quiet and steadfast. Example? We are setting good and healthy boundaries when we simply refuse to engage in a useless argument with a toxic person. Another rea- son setting boundaries is difficult to do? We internally worry that we are withholding forgiveness and staying resentful. Boundaries have nothing to do with forgiveness or resentment. They have everything to do with the quality of our interactions with the people in our lives.

Many survivors will work their way through the first stage of *Despair*, second stage of *Education*, third stage of *Awakening*, and find themselves paralyzed at the fourth stage of *Boundaries*. They don't know where to go from this point. They have enough knowledge to recognize they need to do something big with their situation, but the options completely intimidate them. I have watched some survivors run back to their abusers and try to pretend they don't know it is a harmful environment. Denial is a powerful human component that cannot be ignored in the context of psychological abuse. Ironic, right? Denial is the exact action of ignoring the truth in front of us. Denial demands survivors reject that they are, in fact, experiencing hidden abuse. If survivors choose to stop recovery right here, that is their choice, and we love them just the same. Research shows it takes people many attempts to leave unhealthy relationships. I hope that all survivors feel welcomed in this journey and in the book study groups, regardless of where they are on their path. Those of us in the recovery community are here to support and encourage survivors, not be agents of shame because people are not doing what we think they should with their lives.

For those who are willing to look at what boundaries might be like for their particular situation, let's take a glance at the two types of contact I see most often as a therapist. The first I am going to call Detached Contact, and the second is No Contact.

### Detached Contact

This is exactly as it sounds, and it involves more than just limiting time. It is the posturing of the survivor's heart. There are still interactions between the abuser and the survivor, but the tone is radically different than before

*Detached Contact is about the emotional state of the survivor.*

the abuse was uncovered and understood. Detached Contact is about the emotional state of the survivor. It is entirely up to the survivor to decide what is needed in order to embrace recovery from abuse and remain in some level of contact. Before recovery, the target was tossed to and fro by the abuser.

The hateful words stung deeply and the psychological mind games threw the person into a tailspin. Once recovery starts, a survivor may choose Detached Contact for a variety of reasons. He or she is now fully, completely, and utterly aware of what is being dealt with in the toxic environment. That is a huge shift in power. Detached Contact works in many different life situations. Some survivors even choose to remain in their marriages, but they implement a strategic version of Detached Contact. Education is powerful and can enable survivors to make the right choices for their lives.

Trying to emotionally and physically limit contact is often the first step when I am working with new clients. We try having clients take baby steps away from the abuser to help with the detoxing process. If immediate safety is ever a presenting issue, a slow detox won't work, and getting away is the only option. Honestly, that is not usually the situation when clients come to see me for counseling. The vast majority have the physical and emotional safety to think through their decisions and make plans that are thought out, rather than making knee-jerk responses.

Implementing Detached Contact might begin with something like not returning a toxic person's phone call right away; instead, waiting 30 minutes. Survivors can spend that time working through the anxiety of not jumping when the abuser signals to jump. Starting Detached Contact might include not engaging in any future lengthy personal conversations with a toxic co-worker. Instead the survivor is now keeping the conversations at a surface level. Detached Contact can also look like saying "No" to another volunteer request from an abusive church leader. Small empowering steps towards independence from a psychological abuser are incredibly important to the deprogramming process of recovery. When a survivor can start to gently—but firmly—turn the direction of a toxic relationship, it allows the individual to gain confi-

*Small empowering steps towards independence from a psychological abuser are incredibly important to the deprogramming process of recovery.*

dence. It also helps with the chemical detoxing that must occur when trauma bonding (intermittent reinforcement) has happened in the relationship. Is it possible for survivors to break the emotional chains in which they are enslaved while they remain in contact? Most definitely yes. I see it every day and have for years. Is it a hard road? Undeniably. But so is cutting off immediate contact. There are no easy options when psychological abusers have spread their venom. I want to emphatically say from a mental health perspective, healing can and does occur even while some survivors are still in contact. The key is the level of toxicity of the environment and its impact on the harmed individual. This is why counseling is exceptionally helpful when survivors have very big life decisions to make about toxic relationships.

There is a huge inequality in the level of life upheaval between going No Contact with a boyfriend or girlfriend who does not live in the same home and ending a marriage of thirty-plus years that has children and grandchildren to consider. Likewise, there is a vast difference between someone quitting a job he or she has worked at for five years and another person deciding whether to sell her or his portion of a business because the co-owner is a psychological abuser. I am honestly growing weary of non-mental health professionals stating that having No Contact is the only true form of recovery. It is simply an ill-informed opinion based on their own personal experiences of what worked for them, and they are projecting that onto other people's very different life circumstances. The key to remember is you, the survivor, must sort through all of your options. You lay your head on your pillow at night and have to feel good about your life choices. I do not live in your world, nor do any other advocates in the recovery community. Do what works for you. That may include implementing Detached Contact; but it may not.

Detached Contact is often seen in family relationships. Just because there is an abusive individual (or maybe even a few) in a family, many survivors are not willing to give up contact with their entire extended clan. They may also not want to remove all the relatives from their children's lives. In these situations, survivors are hopeful they can find safe emotional and physical distance through Detached Contact. If not, then having No Contact might be the healthiest option. We will explore that in a moment. If Detached Contact is the goal, exactly how that will look is going to be unique to each situation. When trying to determine the appropriateness of implementing Detached Contact, I often ask the following questions:

- *What has worked in the past?*
- *What has not worked in the past?*
- *At what point does contact start to make you anxious?*
- *Who are the safe people in the environment?*
- *Who are the abusers in the environment?*
- *At the end of the day, what are a few things that would have made it successful?*

- *At the end of the day, what are a few things that would make you very upset if they were to occur?*

Based on the answers to the above questions, a plan for contact can be made. It takes time to perfect Detached Contact, but I have watched survivors do it beautifully. Self-care is always essential if remaining in contact is going to be the choice. Some situations present no choice, such as shared custody with an abuser or an elderly parent who must be cared for, regardless of how the survivor feels about the relationship. Learning how to emotionally detach and being aware of internal dialogue is essential to recovery. Detached Contact is about staying emotionally distant while in the presence of toxic people. It is not about limiting contact and still being overwhelmingly triggered the entire time. If a survivor is experiencing full panic during contact, the momentum of their healing will be impacted. An individual may want to work with a knowledgeable therapist, life coach, or mentor to learn specific tools for his or her personal situation to achieve a healthy level of Detached Contact. It is about learning to take thoughts under control, replace them with healthier internal messages, and establish boundaries

*Detached Contact is about staying emotionally distant while in the presence of toxic people. It is not about limiting contact and still being overwhelmingly triggered the entire time.*

that work in the environment.

As you create your own Detached Contact plan, there are a few things to consider:

- The success of Detached Contact will absolutely be contingent on the level of support you have from healthy people in your life. It is not about the number of individuals who are in your support system, but the quality of those relationships. It is very difficult to reach Detached Contact with a toxic person if you are isolated and have no one cheering you on, loving you well, and helping you find your laughter.

- Detached Contact starts in the survivor's thought life. What we think is what we feel, so survivors must be vigilant to remind themselves that the distorted thinking is coming from the narcissist, sociopath, or psychopath. Fight the urge to internalize all of the blame. The toxic person will try to shift it onto your lap, and you must resist the temptation to receive it. Thoughts such as, "This is his (her) issue, not mine" are helpful as a centering point when the crazy-making behaviors start again, and they always do.

- As I mentioned previously, I like to use the picture of a spotlight. The story goes that a toxic person does or says something ridiculous and the spotlight starts on them. However, if the survivor reacts in anger or another heightened emotion, guess where the spotlight moves? Onto the survivor, and the toxic person loves it. No longer are they dealing with his or her abusive behaviors, but now it's about the survivor. Learning to stay calm and keeping the spotlight on the toxic person is critical to the success of Detached Contact. No one said it was going to be easy, and it's not, but some situations warrant remaining in contact. Survivors must have the skills to be in recovery at the same time.

- Psychological abusers like to reconstruct history. They will take situations from the past, and in the retelling of the story, completely change what actually happened. It can be infuriating for survivors. It will often send them spiraling down emotionally. The key is to not follow the toxic person into their vortex of lies. A survivor in Detached Contact will need to master the skills of calmly, but firmly, pointing out the true story. Say it once, maybe twice, and then be done. In Detached Contact, it is important that survivors call out the toxic person regarding the inconsistencies of their storytelling. Some psychological abusers will rage at a survivor who firmly, but not in anger, talks back to them. If that is your situation, then Detached Contact may not be your safest option. No Contact might be the only choice, and you may need to work with a therapist or life coach to help sort through the situation.

*The key is to not follow the toxic person into their vortex of lies.*

- When a survivor remains steady and is not spun by the actions of the toxic person, it shows the abuser's own "crazy" behaviors much more clearly. Survivors who have mastered the ability to be in control of their emotions are often stunned at how clear life becomes. They are able to recognize the chaos the toxic person creates, and can see exactly the game being played. Survivors often get to a point in recovery where they can predict the responses of the toxic person. No longer are they being emotionally pulled around at the whims of the abuser. The survivor has gained power over their emotional responses. If we don't learn to manage our emotions, someone else will be more than happy to come along and manage them for us— usually a toxic person who wants to pull just the right strings to get the negative response they want out of us. Having self-control is empowering and healing.

- Some toxic people alternate between being pleasant to be around and then to their most awful behaviors. This roller coaster can be very confusing. Survivors may think that the toxic person has changed their ways. If a survivor is going to implement Detached Contact, the best approach is to never forget that the bad days will return. A survivor is most hurt when they think the toxic person is different, but the exact same level of dysfunction returns.

- Detached Contact involves setting firm boundaries that cannot be reneged on by the survivor. The toxic person, or people, must know a survivor means business and will follow through. Example? A survivor can tell a toxic person that if they drink and attempt to drive, the survivor will not be getting in the car with them. Period. The survivor will have a taxi service contact already in her or his phone, and will follow through on taking an alternate ride if the abuser chooses to drink. The toxic person will most likely accuse the survivor of trying to "control" them, but the survivor should reply with something like, "You can choose to drink if you want. I am not saying to not drink. I am saying that if you do, I will not be getting in the car with you. Drink away. No one is stopping you. I will keep myself safe at all times, and that choice is not yours to make." The survivor delivers this message in a firm and clear tone of voice, not mad or screaming. Just stating the facts. Take it or leave it, toxic person.

- Survivors in Detached Contact must come to accept the psychological abuser as they are, not as the survivor wishes. No amount of praying is going to change someone unless they want to be changed. Psychological abusers do not want to be any different because the way they live their lives works for them. Acceptance of who they are, and who they always will be, is vital to finding recovery while in Detached Contact. If you are still hoping, praying, and wishing for a change, then you have not truly reached an awakening yet. No judgment from me because I understand acceptance is hard. Also,

> *The survivor delivers this message in a firm and clear tone of voice, not mad or screaming. Just stating the facts. Take it or leave it, toxic person.*

I am not at all saying that you have to accept abuse as normal. I do not mean acceptance as a replacement for the word "tolerate." What I am saying is that your hope of the person being better someday must come to an abrupt end. When that takes place, a power shift occurs in the relationship. The survivor is now free to see the abuser with clarity. Detached Contact only works where there is clarity of mind within the survivor.

As you can see, Detached Contact is not the easy road. I often compare Detached Contact and having No Contact to addiction recovery. Having No Contact is the equivalent of choosing to never drink alcohol or use drugs again. Former addicts or alcoholics can live the rest of their lives and never touch another drink, drug, or pill. It is physically possible. Survivors of psychological abuse can cut ties with their abusers, heal, and never look back. However, having Detached Contact is similar to recovering from an eating disorder. No one can survive without food. Individuals must face and manage their drug of choice (food) at least three times each and every day. Both roads of recovery are admirable and individually hard. Through No Contact, survivors can find ever-increasing distance from the malice that almost permanently ruined their lives. The other journey, Detached Contact, is the consistent process of living lives of healing while still facing their antagonists, but with limited emotional engagement. As you can see, having No Contact turns out to be the path that allows more distance from abusive experiences. I am sure this is why many advocates in the psychological abuse recovery community have such strong opinions about it. However, tell that to a courageous person who faces her or his eating disorder every day, or to a survivor who must (or chooses to) use Detached Contact. Some recovery situations just do not get a clean break.

## No Contact

Now we are at the point where cutting ties with psychological abusers is the best option for some survivors' situations. While this path has its own set of challenges, once the removal of toxicity has occurred and the dust has settled, having No Contact is the most concrete way of moving forward and away from abuse. At some point along the timeline of being in contact with a narcissist, sociopath, or psychopath, many survivors will come to a place where they recognize that the toxic person provides no value to their life. Toxic people have a way of completely wearing out their welcome. It is at this point a survivor will begin the process of cutting contact and refusing to be a pawn in the abusive game. Psychological abusers do not realize that people authentically grown weary of their ridiculousness, find recovery from the abuse, and eventually move on without looking back.

If your life circumstances allow you to have No Contact, and you find that is the best answer for your personal journey, then there are a few things to consider:

- You will be tempted to break your No Contact decision. Be prepared when those days arrive. Yes, I said days because it won't be just one-and-done. Have a safety plan ready. It might include calling a fellow survivor for support.

- Many abusers try to Hoover their targets back into conversations. Remember, Hoovering is when toxic people decide to pop back up in the lives of survivors. They come back around making promises they will not, cannot, and have no intention of keeping. The Hoovering is done just to reinforce their belief that they still have the survivor under their control and within reach whenever they darn well want.

- Some Hoovering is done—not with promises of love or a better relationship—but it comes in the form of stirring up an argument or some drama to pull the survivor back into contact. In the research project Dr. John and I completed, most survivors who responded shared that their Hoovering experiences were very unpleasant. The abuser pushed just the right buttons to try and get the survivor to re-engage in argumentative contact.

- Not all abusers Hoover. Confusing, I know. Some do. Some don't. If you decide to implement No Contact and do not experience outright Hoovering, expect the toxic person to show off publicly in some manner. One of their favorite tools is social media because they can present a calculated version of themselves. They will attempt to make their post-you life look as perfect and gloriously happy as possible. It is vitally important to remember that psychological abusers never change. Toxic people will simply replay the Idealize-Devalue-Discard song again with new targets. Showing off to harm survivors who have decided to go No Contact does not happen just with former romantic partners. It occurs in various relationships, like at work or at church.

- As the distance grows between you and the abuser, you will start to doubt yourself. Human nature is that time does not heal all wounds, but it does have a way of softening the memories. That is how we can go through embarrassing or frightening life events and later find ourselves retelling the stories with humor. The memories of connections with abusers are similar. As time goes on, you may find yourself slipping in your conviction that having No Contact was warranted. Keeping a journal or a No Contact list is very helpful when you need a quick reminder of why cutting ties was the only good option. I have been known to suggest that people put a picture collage of the positive symbols of their post-abuse life on their phone backgrounds. This serves as a reminder of what they

*I have been known to suggest that people put a picture collage of the positive symbols of their post-abuse life on their phone backgrounds. This serves as a reminder of what they are fighting to protect by remaining No Contact.*

are fighting to protect by remaining No Contact.

- You will need to create a new life. It may mean finding a new group of friends, a new church, a new home, a new place of employment, or a new romantic interest. Maybe all of them, depending on how much damage was done to your life by the abuser. The timing of the arrival of these new places and people in your life is very individual. Going No Contact is always about leaving something harmful behind to either live without it in the future or replace with a healthier option. It is a process, so be patient with yourself as you get back up from having been repeatedly and intentionally emotionally knocked down and kicked.
- Ending a relationship always involves walking away from positive aspects of the other person. If it was awful all the time, breaking up would be easy. Grieving what was good is part of being ready to go No Contact.

Regardless of whether survivors have Detached Contact or No Contact, one of the main hindrances of recovery is rewiring the repetitious lies of the abuser. Psychological abusers use brainwashing techniques to embed certain ideas in their targets. Thoughts like:

- You'll end up alone.
- This job is the only path to reach your career goals.
- This church is the only one God is really using in a dynamic way to do His will.
- Your family will always be there for you, but friends

*Unraveling the lies and replacing them with truth is at the heart of the recovery journey for survivors of psychological abuse.*

come and go.

Unraveling the lies and replacing them with truth is at the heart of the recovery journey for survivors of psychological abuse. If you are finding it difficult to sort through *Stage Four: Boundaries*, try not to get discouraged. If at all possible, find a therapist for at least a few sessions. If you cannot do that, go to the *Resources* section in the back of this book and find an online support group. Perhaps finding a local book study of this book is a healthy choice for you. (www. healingfromhiddenabuse.com). Please keep doing what you can to sift through your options. I know it is a hard stage. Your wholeness demands that you figure out how to either implement Detached Contact or have No Contact. There just are no other options in the world of psychological abuse recovery.

# STAGE FIVE: RESTORATION

𝖂

*After a survivor of psychological abuse has identified their Despair (Stage One), Educated themselves on the specifics of psychological abuse (Stage Two), had an Awakening that recovery is possible (Stage Three), and implemented Boundaries (Stage Four), the next stage is the Restoration of the material items, life event moments, financial stability, physical health, mental health, or any other losses the survivor identifies as having been stolen during the season of abuse. This should be an encouraging stage as survivors start to tangibly see the fruits of their recovery work. Restoration can take longer than survivors expect so patience with the process of recovery is vitally important. Without patience, a survivor can become easily discouraged.*

One of the first signs that survivors have reached this stage in recovery is when they feel the desire to spend their free time on activities unrelated to recovery education. Survivors describe entering this stage as having come to a point of saturation regarding all the new knowledge they have found for themselves. Often, people long to pull away from the online forums and other reading materials about narcissism, sociopathy, and psychopathy. This is not a rejection of the people or experiences survivors have enjoyed in order to find healing; it is actually a positive indicator that normalcy is returning. Maybe it is occurring for the first time, as in the case of childhood abuse. Survivors in this stage of recovery feel an attraction to new hobbies and ways to enrich their lives. This longing is wonderful and can serve as a catalyst for fresh adventures.

One of the main roadblocks to *Stage Five: Restoration* is either the conscious or subconscious belief that if you start to really live again, maybe you are letting the abuser off the hook. It is as if in your suffering you are showing yourself, your abuser, and the world the truth of the damage done to you. I completely understand the source of this thinking. In some ways, it makes sense. When something has been destroyed, the rubble sits there as a monument to the destruction, not unlike a burned-out building or a damaged car after an accident. The item reflects the hot flames that consumed everything in its path. It shows all the scratches, broken glass, and crushed metal. To allow the building or the car to remain in their damaged condition would be to leave the injury visible for everyone to see. Eventually though, the building must be rebuilt and the car either repaired or sent to the junk yard. One way or another, life does move on.

In the case of recovery from psychological abuse, at some point, survivors must choose to live again. They will have to work through the internal messages that rattle around keeping them stuck in their charred or crushed state of mind. To move into restoration does not mean the abusers never did anything wrong. Moving forward is also not an indicator that their actions never harmed you. What restoration does is provide the ability for survivors to bring hope back into their lives; maybe for the first time.

The important thing to remember is that even if survivors stayed broken for the rest of their lives, the abusers do not. They are not experiencing the same devastation. They never did. They immediately moved on in their lives because they lack any authentic connection to anyone. Cutting fraudulent ties and moving on was easy for them. Your need to remain visibly harmed in some effort to show the world what was done to you really is the notorious idea of drinking poison to harm someone else. There is absolutely nothing redeemable about subconsciously refusing to heal and move forward. Living well does not mean the abuse never happened. It means the abuse did not damage you beyond repair. That is a great message for any abuser to witness. The toxic person who harmed you may never see you living a good post-abuse life, but you will. Once you go through the *Restoration* stage, you will know your life is no longer controlled by an abuser. You might actually start to believe better days are ahead. You know what, my friend?

They are, and I am excited for you.

This is the stage where individuals are allowed to start dreaming. They have walked the road of recovery enough to begin adding back what was robbed during the abuse. No longer are they in the process of living one day at a time, but are healed at a level that they now desire true restoration. They ache for newness and vibrancy. Survivors who reach *Restoration* seek to have any holes left by their abusers filled. For far too many seasons, survivors had things stolen and destroyed in their lives. Sometimes literally. I want you to see the *Restoration* stage as a chance to dream and dream big! It does not mean things will come quickly. They won't. But they will never come if you do not identify, at a micro level, the parts of you that are still missing. Some things can never be specifically replaced, but there are many other ways to experience the joys of restoration.

Go ahead and get comfortable. If you're a tea drinker, get yourself a cup. Breathe and relax. As we start thinking about the areas that need restoration in your life, I do not want it to become a burdensome to-do list. It is not meant for you to be bogged down by this stage. Hope is the theme of *Stage Five*. All things becoming new is the spirit of *Stage Five*. If you find yourself slipping into perfectionism or impatience, put the book aside for a few hours (or days). It will still be here when you return. For everything there is

> *Hope is the theme of* Stage Five. *All things becoming new is the spirit of* Stage Five.

a season. Restoration should come at the time when it can be life-giving, not overwhelming.

Some of the common areas that many survivors see as needing restoration include:

- Enjoyment of holidays, vacations, and other celebrations.
- Financial stability: paying off debts and increasing savings.
- Restoration of physical health: enjoying consistent energy levels, reduction in body pain, and other ailments.
- Restoration of emotional well-being: living free—or significantly reduced levels—of anxiety, worry, and depression.
- Replacement of material items destroyed or stolen during the abuse.

Survivors cannot get back the actual hours and days that were taken from them during their abuse, but the themes of the missing items can be redeemed. I like that word, "redeemed." One of its meanings is, "to make something that is bad, unpleasant, etc. better or more acceptable." If a target of psychological abuse never goes through the purposeful efforts to redeem what was lost, it remains an untied transition. There is no closure. What was lost just lays there on the ground, having been stomped on by the toxic person. It will never be brought back to life and I find that tragic. Of all the offenses an abuser puts a target through, I am most deeply outraged by the stealing of goodness. It offends me at a core level. How dare someone think they can waltz into a life and start destroying aspects of it? The sheer arrogance is staggering.

Let's take a look at some specific examples of restoration, and how redemption can come to areas of a survivor's life:

**Enjoyment of holidays, vacations, and other celebrations.**

Survivors wonder why toxic people chronically ruin vacations, holidays, and other special life moments. As with all psychological abuse recovery, no one specific answer fits every situation. There are a few theories to ponder as to why survivors may have experienced unpleasant holidays and other celebrations while with the abusers. Narcissists, sociopaths, and psychopaths are attachment disordered. Therefore, they are uncomfortable with periods of relationship closeness. They intentionally cause negative chaos to create emotional distance between themselves and others. Vacations require teamwork and mutual cooperation. Toxic people do not possess either of these relational skills, and they are not willing to learn them. When things don't go their way, they have no guilt causing stress. This is true even while on vacation or on days like birthdays, Thanksgiving, or Christmas. No day is sacred to them. Any occasion is open game for them to ruin with an adult temper tantrum. If special events do not revolve around the abuser, they cannot tolerate attention going elsewhere. They will intentionally ruin the day. Abusive people cannot set aside their own frustrations in order for others to enjoy the special moments. They allow their unmanaged moods to spill out and taint what could have been good memories for other people. They even do this to their own children.

*When things don't go their way, they have no guilt causing stress. This is true even while on vacation or on days like birthdays, Thanksgiving, or Christmas. No day is sacred to them. Any occasion is open game for them to ruin with an adult temper tantrum.*

What can you do to bring restoration to this area of your life story? If you have established Detached Contact, it may mean having a separate celebration that does not include the abuser. Even if that celebration is treating yourself to a small gift, taking yourself out to lunch somewhere you have wanted to try, or buying yourself a bouquet of flowers to enjoy. Just because someone else refuses to celebrate our life milestones and victories does not mean we should treat special occasions as unworthy. When we don't honor ourselves, we are coming into agreement with the abuser's toxic agenda. We end up abusing ourselves too.

While with the toxic person, perhaps you had multiple vacations ruined. Maybe it happened so often that even though you now have No Contact, you are still turned off to the idea of taking a vacation. One of the lingering wounds of psychological abuse is that many survivors struggle with symptoms that fit the criteria for diagnosis of Post-Traumatic Stress Disorder (PTSD). The avoidance of places and memories that trigger unpleasant responses are a part of the disorder. If you find yourself hesitant—or outright afraid—to try a full vacation post abuse, perhaps book a night or two in a hotel in your local area and have a "staycation." There are wonderful deals to be found online for hotels, especially last-minute trips. Pack your swimsuit and head off to enjoy the amenities the hotel has to offer. If it is in the budget, order room service. If not, dash out and grab some of your favorite food. After you return to your room, take your meal, pile up on the comfy bed, and soak in all the calmness a life of recovery has offered you. Enjoy your hotel picnic. Pause to take in the fact that no man-child or woman-child is there to start a fight for absolutely no apparent reason. There are no drama queens (or kings) there to make it all about them and their endless demands. No, you are there to redeem your enjoyment of time away from the routine of life. You are there to heal. Can staying in a hotel in your own town be healing? Yes. This is true because you will be living in the opposite spirit in which the psychological abuser wanted you to live during your time together. The abuser wanted you drained, anxious, and catering to his or her needs. But look at you. You're not doing any of that nonsense.

You're enjoying an evening away and resting in the fruits of your labor. It may be by yourself, with your kids, or with a friend. It doesn't matter. By taking small, safe steps towards an area that once was off limits because of an abuser, you are rewiring your subconscious to know this is now a safe activity, minus Donnie or Debbie Downer (aka the abuser).

If you have implemented Detached Contact with your abuser and travel is a part of your plan, there are ways for you to also enjoy restoration in this area. As you plan your next vacation, make a list of your hopes during the time away. The key is to keep the list to the things in which you actually have control. You will never have control over the abuser's moods. However, you can decide you will enjoy being away from work for a few days, noticing the moment the plane's wheels lift off the runway, or finding one space in each vacation day to be aware of the small joys in your life. There are ways to avoid getting hooked into the circular fights that happen with a toxic person. Using your skills to disengage from conflict during a vacation will make things go smoother for yourself. Enjoying moments of solitude will absolutely help with your patience levels and give a probably much needed break. Many survivors choose not to take a seven day or longer vacation when in Detached Contact. Why? It is simply too long of a time to be in close quarters with a toxic person. Shorter—four or five day trips—might work better to help keep life smoother and focused on the "vacation high" that is present at the beginning of any trip. For many people, day six or seven are when the wheels start to fall off and toxic people return to their baseline obnoxious selves. The solution? Go on shorter trips, and plan for self-care while away. What works for you might be different than the next person, so take the time to individualize your own plan.

## Financial stability: paying off debts and increasing savings.

Financial abuse is real and takes one of two forms. The first is when a toxic person intentionally creates financial dependency for the survivor in order to have a deeper level of control over her or him. The toxic person may either outright sabotage a survivor from gaining financial independence, or under the guise of being caring, the toxic person will make it so the survivor is dependent. Financial independence from a narcissist, sociopath, or psychopath is a key factor to a survivor finding freedom. It will look different for each situation, but the common thread is survivors knowing they can financially support themselves if needed. The second form of financial abuse is perpetrated when an abuser has an overdeveloped sense of entitlement. Financial abuse can come from a toxic individual who purposefully creates a reliance on the survivor to meet the toxic person's financial needs as an obligation of the relationship. Example? When an abusive spouse refuses to work even though the financial need is obvious or the burden is too great for one person. A toxic person has no issue using others, and with little to no regard for the well-being of the survivor. This form of abuser will use his or her spouse as an economic machine and supply source, rather than a beloved partner in creating a healthy financial life together.

Restoration in the area of finances will be very specific to what the survivor sees as redeeming. I would encourage you to make a list of the financial concerns you may have from the abuse season. As you look at the list, think about very small steps in the right direction that you can begin taking. The goal here is to move forward. Digging out of financial abuse or mismanagement takes a long time for most people. The key is getting started and walking slowly to where you want to be. Example? If you need to establish more savings, go online and open a free account with one of the banking or investment companies. Some accounts are very quick to open and easy to understand. Look at your current budget, and start an auto-draft into your new savings or investment account. It does not matter if your auto-draft is $10 a month. Start somewhere. There is

> *The goal here is to move forward. Digging out of financial abuse or mismanagement takes a long time for most people. The key is getting started and walking slowly to where you want to be.*

something magical that happens when we begin moving forward. Momentum kicks in and good things happen. You've started moving and you are going forward! That's exciting.

**Restoration of physical health: enjoying consistent energy levels, reduction in body pain, and other ailments.**

There are biological shifts that take place when involved in a psychologically abusive environment. Those changes intensely influence the overall physical wellness of the survivor. The body can only take on a limited amount of stress before it starts shutting down in response to the abuse. This is when being in "Exposed Contact" (pre-recovery contact) with a toxic person starts to literally destroy the survivor. I call it exposed contact because there was no armor on to protect the survivor. She or he was exceptionally vulnerable and an open target to harm. Being exposed allows all of the poison to reach the survivor. It should serve as a serious red flag when the relationship starts taking a toll on the survivor's health. Many people have had to deal with autoimmune problems, eating disorders, chronic inflammation, and a whole host of other physical manifestations of the abuse. In order for the *Restoration* stage to have an impact on survivors, they must take an honest account of the damage done to them. We cannot recover from something we will not admit is a problem. What within your own health has been affected by the abuse? Recovery is a great time to complete a full physical assessment and include a comprehensive blood count panel. When clients come to my office and are struggling with depressive symptoms, I always ask if they have had a recent doctor's appointment. If not, I encourage them to get one right away. Thyroid issues can often mimic depressive symptoms, and we do not want to try and treat a physical condition through mental health services, and vice versa. If there are no underlying medical concerns, we know the specific work that must be done to heal from psychological abuse.

Symptoms of inflammatory disorders, such as fibromyalgia, are common among survivors. Inflammation happens when the immune system turns on the body. Of course, that's a non-medically trained description. If you find yourself suffering from chronic body pain, digestive issues, migraines, or other physical symptoms, please take care of yourself. If you are like me and not a huge fan of the Western medical model, make an appointment with whichever health practitioner fits into your belief system about health. I know many survivors who have had wonderful experiences with acupuncture, chiropractic care, and massage therapy for post-abuse recovery.

I am a huge advocate of regular exercise, and it does not have to be two hours every day with a trainer. Actually, it is better if it is not that intense. What survivor new to recovery has enough energy for a two-hour daily workout? Nobody that I know. Early on in recovery, exercise is best when it is not draining, but gets the body moving and good brain chemistry flowing. Consider exercising for a shorter period of time such as twenty minutes. The reason heavy workouts are not helpful in the beginning is because most survivors of psychological abuse are beyond drained emotionally and physically. One person described it as if all the energy from the body had been quietly drained out the bottom of their feet. No one could see it, but they were being completely emptied nonetheless. At the beginning of recovery, there is not much left in the energy tank. Exhaustion doesn't even begin to describe the feeling. Activities that zap what little reserves a survivor is building back up are counterproductive to the task of eventually filling the individual with a normal amount of vibrancy.

*Activities that zap what little reserves a survivor is building back up are counterproductive to the task of eventually filling the individual with a normal amount of vibrancy.*

I personally love hot yoga (but not that really hot serious kind). I am talking about the more moderate—"stretch and breathe"—type of yoga. Some people enjoy swimming. Others need to get out on the road and run a couple of miles. Whatever you choose to do, be as consistent about it as you can. Check in with your healthcare provider to make sure there are no limitations specific to you. If you're not currently working out, set the goal of doing something once this week. That's it. Just one time and next week, try exercising twice. The week after, three times. Stay with three times a week until your energy levels are consistently closer to what you view as healthy and normal. A survivor cannot give at the gym what is not in his or her energy tank. Otherwise, you are depleting what little reserves that are trying to be built. In addition, the brain chemistry benefits of low-to-moderate exercise can sometimes be the difference between needing an anti-anxiety and anti-depressant medication, or not. The medications are a valuable help to many people, and that is exactly what they are designed to be. If you can get the emotional lift you need through exercise, even better. Depending on the intensity of the abuse, survivors frequently need a combination of treatments in order to feel well again. That is a great path for a season.

**Restoration of emotional well-being: living free—or significantly reduced levels—of anxiety, worry, and depression.**

A target of psychological abuse should be cautious if she or he has previously dealt with depressive symptoms. Why? The adrenaline rushes that come from being in a toxic relationship can temporarily mask depressive, low moods. How does this happen? When an abuser is love bombing, or creating other forms of emotional chaos, a survivor's energy increases as the level of adrenaline increases. This inevitably creates a biochemical dependency on the toxic relationship to lift the survivor out of a flat mood. However, the fall from an abuse-induced high is always much lower than a survivor expects. This is why the *Restoration* stage of recovery is critical to the emotional well-being of the survivor. The body must recalibrate and that can be a slow process. I am sure you wish that I could give you a magic formula to get through this quicker. I promise that if I knew one, I would gladly share it. "One foot in front of the other" is the surest way I know how to walk out of the confusion of psychological abuse.

As the process of recovery continues, individuals find methods of enriching their emotional health that are personal to them. The key to this section of the *Restoration* stage is to find what works for you. In the past, what has helped to navigate through the wide range of emotions that come up in daily life? Do what works and avoid what doesn't. I know that sounds ridiculously simple, but I am shocked at how many times we all repeatedly do things that do not enrich our lives. We go on autopilot and stay in the vicious cycle of circling the same metaphorical mountain but actually go nowhere. This stage is not the time for repetitious habits that do not work to better our lives.

Restoration of peace of mind is very individual. You will need to spend more time reflecting on what it will look like specifically for you. Will you be able to find joy in things you didn't before? Perhaps you will notice yourself laughing from a place that is more authentic and rich. Maybe the deep darkness that was present during the *Despair* stage will now be mixed with moments of sparkle and joy. *Restoration* of emotional health will come in waves of freshness. If cultivated, the better days will begin to overtake those heavy, soul-crushing days. *Restoration* is a wonderful stage for survivors.

### The replacement of material items destroyed or stolen during the abuse.

I have yet in this book to get personal about my journey as a survivor. Oh, maybe you thought I was just a therapist who specializes in the area of psychological abuse? No, my friend. I am in this same boat as you. I have shared "My Story" on my website (www.shannonthomas.com). You are welcome to go take a look. For now, I want to talk about my own experience with restoration of material items destroyed.

I was eleven years old when my beloved dad was violently killed in our home during a home invasion. It's a long story, and maybe someday I will share the details in another book. For today, let's just say my life after my dad died was very unpleasant. That is an incredible understatement, but the details are not important for right now. I am an only child and after his passing, I remained in the care of my mom. She battled intense personality disorder characteristics and substance abuse issues. In 2004 she passed away, and at that point I had been estranged from her for many years. In fact, I was informed of her passing when law enforcement contacted me, because I was living several states away from her region. Going No Contact with my mom was the only way for me to even remotely begin to heal from the overwhelming amount of chronic turmoil she stirred up wherever she went. At one point in my late twenties, I was granted a restraining order to keep myself safe from her. You know the wheels of the maternal cart have hurled off when your own adult daughter is granted a three-year stay away order. I slept slightly better with the protective order in place, but for years I always had my pepper spray out and unlocked as I climbed the outside flight of stairs leading to the front door of my apartment. She was violent, and given the unsolved nature of my father's death decades earlier, local law enforcement felt it necessary to advise me about how to keep myself safe.

*At one point in my late twenties, I was granted a restraining order to keep myself safe from her. You know the wheels of the maternal cart have hurled off when your own adult daughter is granted a three-year stay away order.*

My dad was a high school cross-country and track coach. I grew up with a stop watch in my hand and timed student runners as they trained on my father's numerous school teams. He was awarded "Coach of the Year" in several districts, and running culture is a part of my best childhood memories. I was a distance runner as well. Prior to his death, I had the opportunity to race in a regional Junior Olympics qualifier meet. I recall getting lost on the race path. I think I may have come in last place during that meet, but my dad was very gracious and the ever positive coach. For my efforts in becoming a qualifier for the cross-country meet, I was awarded a medal. It was a Junior Olympic medal and I cherished it. I kept it in the plastic box it came in, and for years, I would show it to everyone who visited. After my dad's death, that medal became even more special to me. I won't bore you with too many of the details here, but life with mom was rough. The really awful sort of rough. I think we moved 16 times in 14 years, or something close to those numbers. With each move, I always packed my own room, and that Junior Olympic medal was personally kept with me during each transition. I did not want to lose it.

As an adult, I don't have that medal anymore because a year or two after my dad's death, and during one of her rage episodes, my mom flushed it down the toilet in an attempt to emotionally harm me. I am not even sure how it made its way through the plumbing in our house—given its weight—but I can still picture her tearing through my room, taking the medal off my shelf, and blowing out of my room in a fury of dysfunction. The next thing I heard was the toilet flushing. I ran into the bathroom and she screamed in my face that it was gone. Gone?! I was devastated. Over the years, I came to have most of my possessions destroyed by her out-of-control, abusive hands. Those hands caused a lot of damage in my life following the death of my father.

Fast forward to adult life: I still enjoy running and guess what? Many of the 5k, 10k, and longer runs also hand out medals for finishers. Now in my forties, that shiny medal at the end of the race is often my only motivation to finish! In 2010 I ran a half marathon, and the medal I received that day is among my most loved belongings. I am sure you can understand the significance for me; yet, there is even more to the story. During the years following my dad's death, food had become a safe escape for me. Since my twenties, I have lost over 120lbs. Slowly losing the weight over many years culminated in my finishing a half marathon and getting the finisher's medal. It represents hours of training and pushing through intense fears. Whenever we face our past wounds, fear will be there whispering all the reasons we should not even try. Running that long race forced me to face many old demons. Not only did I face them, but I became a conqueror of them as well.

*Whenever we face our past wounds, fear will be there whispering all the reasons we should not even try.*

Today, that half marathon race medal is in a shadow box with my race number behind it, and they hang on the wall of my peaceful, calm adult home. No one is going to destroy it. It will not be ripped off the wall and flushed down the toilet. It is mine to enjoy and look at fondly. That is how restoration works in recovery from psychological abuse. I will never get back my childhood medal and everything it meant to me, but I can replace it with new races and new memories. As an incredibly sweet side note, my child also happens to be a runner. Now we enter 5k races together and are collecting our medals as mom and child. Because of the work I have done in my own recovery, my beloved baby will never endure the flushing of a hard-earned race medal. Instead, we are creating wonderful memories that are a part of redeeming what an abuser had done to me earlier in my life.

What material items do you need restored and redeemed? Did you have a beloved pet your abuser demanded be given away? Did you have a strong sense of fashion your abuser manipulated you into changing, and you are reminded every time you look in your closet? Did you once have a piece of artwork that was meaningful? Please think of one or two items that meant something to you but were lost during the season of abuse. Make a plan to find a way to redeem those items in a manner that brings a smile to your face. Trust me when I say, it makes a difference in recovery.

Will you be able to restore all things? Sadly, no. There are just some items, memories, or days we can never get back. I have lived my entire adult life without any surrogate parents. There have been mentors and older friends who have wandered onto my life path, and mine onto theirs, but none stayed for any length of time. I used to pray and long for a mom or dad figure to come into my life and fill the very deep holes that had been left behind. As I have now reached my mid-forties, I no longer yearn for those relationships in the same way I did a decade or two ago. I am sure you can think of something you wish you were able to restore, but it has yet to come to fruition. Life may be asking you to live without some things and that is when grieving occurs. The point of *Stage Five: Restoration* is to take the actions that are within our power to restore what our abusers took from us. There will be items that we can do nothing about, and that is a stark reality we must come to accept as we move through the stages of recovery.

> *The point of Stage Five: Restoration is to take the actions that are within our power to restore what our abusers took from us.*

# STAGE SIX: MAINTENANCE

❦

*After a survivor of psychological abuse has identified their Despair (Stage One), Educated themselves on the specifics of psychological abuse (Stage Two), had an Awakening that recovery is possible (Stage Three), implemented Boundaries (Stage Four), and experienced Restoration of losses during the abuse (Stage Five), the final stage of recovery from psychological abuse is Maintenance. During this sixth and last stage, survivors will often willingly loop back to earlier stages and experience deeper levels of healing. The Maintenance stage also involves being able to experience healthy relationships going forward and identify toxic people quicker than previously. Maintenance is when a survivor fully lives their life of recovery with the confidence and skills to keep themselves safe from future abuse.*

Welcome, friend, to the last stage of recovery! Does that mean you now will never struggle with post-traumatic stress symptoms, never think of the abuser, and will always run through the hills singing songs of ju-

*You have made it to a very high mountain top, so please slow down enough to enjoy the view. The air is fresher here and your senses are heightened.*

bilance? Of course not. You have made it to a very high mountain top, so please slow down enough to enjoy the view. The air is fresher here and your senses are heightened. This is the point in the journey of healing from psychological abuse that dedicating yourself to living clean becomes the new norm. When you have traveled the journey you have, and fought to find peace, you are less likely to go back to the pits of despair. I saw a quote that said, "When we know how to be happy, we won't tolerate being around someone who makes us unhappy." That is the truth.

At this stage in the process, some survivors are accused of being too rigid or guarded. Generally, I do not think that is true at all. Survivors who struggled through the rough terrain to reach the mountain top have become selective about whom they want around them. Not all people we meet deserve to be in our inner circles. Survivors have worked way too hard to develop clean living to then allow unhealthy people to remain in close proximity. Those two worlds do not go together. An individual doesn't even have to be "toxic" to be undeserving of a place in your life. Access to you is a gift. The ability to call you, text you, e-mail you, see you, come to your home, and basically share space in your life is earned, not easily given. At least it should be. It is yours to parcel out as you choose.

The psychological abuser figuratively kicked down the door of your life. Then, in their rage, they damaged the sacred space of your home. Once their whirlwind of damage came to an end, you got busy with the tasks of cleaning up the debris. You put a fresh coat of paint on the walls, bought new furniture, and hung pictures. It is now a safe space and you feel satisfied. Tell me, why would you allow access to someone with a propensity for damage? You wouldn't. Your healing is yours to guard and yours to enjoy. This is how survivors who have progressed through the six stages of recovery should govern their lives. It is not dependent on whether they are in Detached Contact or No Contact. An educated survivor can, and will, guard against future abuse. How do I know this? Because I watch it happen time and time again. Is it easy? Not at all. Does life get messy sometimes, and the house need to be tidied up again? Sure. That is radically different than allowing an abusive tornado in human form to blow through a survivor's life again.

What skills are needed to continue in this final stage of recovery? It is critical that all survivors learn to take their thoughts captive and shift away from thinking patterns that drag them back into old habits. One of the most common ways survivors sabotage their stability in *Maintenance* is by allowing themselves to focus their thoughts on the fleeting positive moments of the relationship. Often, a survivor will return in their memory to what was but has not been for a long time. In order for healing to be sustained, a balanced view of the relationship must be maintained. It is not about holding on to hurts but not allowing time or distance to distort the truth about the abuse.

If you have implemented Detached Contact, the final stage of recovery can be difficult because toxic people are not toxic every day. They have their good moments too, and those can be confusing for a survivor. Remember, no matter how pleasant a toxic person may behave for a short period of time, they will always return to their baseline abusive behaviors. Example? A psychological abuser may go through a time when—for their own self-interests—they act slightly nicer to those around them. This change often happens after they have been caught in a lie or obvious harm to others. The length of their "dog house" attitude varies from toxic person to toxic person. Eventually, they will shift back to their normal abusive ways. *Maintenance* for those in Detached Contact will include never forgetting the journey you have taken to find healing and keeping it well guarded. The quality of your life depends on your commitment to your recovery.

No Contact will allow survivors to move forward from a particular abuser, but that does not automatically mean you are safe from future abusers. Always have your tool box ready and full of assessment skills, boundaries, and the ability to cut contact with any suspected abusers. *Maintenance* can be tricky when living in No Contact because sometimes the lack of contact was implemented by the abuser through a discard. When that occurs, survivors will need to gain the skill set to walk away from any future abusers. Without the ability to exercise the internal emotional muscle of willfully leaving a harmful environment, survivors are vulnerable to falling into a codependent trap in the future. Having the ability to say "No more" and then follow through by removing themselves from the environment is a necessity to a life of recovery from psychological abuse.

A key component to *Maintenance* is recognizing that you are a new person. You have grown, changed, and are an improved version of yourself. Hopefully that trajectory of healthy living will continue upward. It is important to see yourself in the newness that is now yours. There are sad consequences if we do not recognize that our old selves have

*There are sad consequences if we do not recognize that our old selves have faded away. Insecurity will drive us to push away happy, successful people because we do not think we deserve their attention. Our inner dialogue and self-worth will determine the type of people we allow—or reject—in our lives.*

faded away. Insecurity will drive us to push away happy, successful people because we do not think we deserve their attention. Our inner dialogue and self-worth will determine the type of people we allow—or reject—in our lives. If we don't believe we deserve things like real love, peace of mind, and hope, we will subconsciously sabotage ourselves. We will wonder why we never have them in our life. We can live aimlessly and keep being drawn to the same type of unhealthy people. Instead, we need to fully see that we are different and improved individuals. A new group of people will be attracted to us as well.

As an example, for years after losing the significant amount of weight, I kept buying the wrong size of clothing. It took a gentle prod from a close friend who flat out told me I was dressed in clothing too big. She strongly encouraged me to go to the store with her and try on what she believed was the right size. This friend had worked in the fashion retail industry for years so she knew she was correct in her assessment of me being stuck in an old thinking pattern. Much to my surprise that day, I fit into pants two sizes smaller. I literally was shocked. Due to my past, I did not see myself in my new body, but my friend did. I am here to tell you, my friend, that if you have gone through the six stages of recovery, you are no longer going to "fit" into the old group of people that you once did. That is a good thing. Let healthier people come into your life. You've done the hard work to attract peers who are similar to the new you.

As we conclude our time together, this is a great journaling exercise: Ask yourself the question, "What is a high-quality life for me?" This question is not about what other people think your life should look like or you trying to keep up with anyone else's life. This is a deeply personal and individual question. Often times, people will include living in a way that has a redemptive quality from past experiences. Example? For an adult survivor of childhood abuse, a high-quality life might include parenting in a way that breaks the family tradition of abuse. For another person, it may be related to maintaining his or her financial stability because that goal was not previously reached. As you answer the question, be as specific and detailed as you can. This exercise should serve as a tool of hope and perhaps gratitude for what is already present in your life.

Thank you for spending this time with me, and allowing us to walk through the stages together. I know I have not covered every nuance of psychological abuse recovery. That would be nearly impossible to do in one book. Please take a look at the *Resources* section in the back of this book. There are some amazing people doing work that can benefit you and from which I personally continue to learn from as well. You may also consider taking time to answer the *Personal Reflections* questions at the back of this book. They will serve as reinforcement and help you to personalize all the stages we have gone through together. You may want to look into a local book study group at www.healingfromhiddenabuse.

com. Maybe you feel drawn to being a study host and leader.

I hope you will return to this book as needed, and each time you do, my prayer for you is that a new sweetness enriches your recovery. Always remember that being a target of psychological abuse was not your fault. You did not attract it into your life. You never wanted what was done to you. Now is your time to take what you have learned, maintain your personal healing, and help other people who need the knowledge you now possess deep within you.

Keep dreaming big!

Shannon

# FAMILY AND FRIENDS:
## YOUR LOVED ONE ISN'T CRAZY

I originally wrote this blog in 2015. I am happy that it has been well-received on my website. I want to share it here in case you have family members or friends who might not read the entire book (or any other book really), but need a quick recap of why recovery from psychological abuse is often a long road. I am going to publish the blog in its entirety. The feedback I received from survivors, family members, and friends showed me that it had a positive impact. I hope that will be the same for those in your life who need to read it.

A Letter to Family and Friends:

### Family & Friends: Your Loved One Isn't Crazy

From reading the title, you might be wondering what this post is going to be about. I am writing this for the family and friends of survivors of psychological abuse. Why? Because I hear from many survivors who say that it is incredibly hard for them to describe the insidiousness of the abuse they experienced. Many family and friends just don't know how to support their loved one through the steps of recovery. There is so much to be said on this topic, but I am going to try and just hit the highlights.

For those who aren't familiar with me, I am a licensed clinical social worker supervisor and I am the owner/lead therapist of a private practice. One area of my counseling work includes specializing in recovery from psychological abuse from a narcissist, sociopath, or psychopath (aka toxic person). These relationships can either be romantic, family members, friends, in a work environment, or religious setting. For the purposes of today, I am going to focus on recovery from abuse within a romantic relationship.

October is Domestic Violence Awareness month and if your loved one was romantically connected with a toxic person, he or she was the victim of abuse. I know that may be hard to comprehend because the type of abuse your loved one experienced didn't leave visible bruises or broken bones. It did, however, leave your loved one very harmed and much different from when they began the relationship with the abuser. You may even have witnessed behaviors from your loved one that you never thought she or he would do. Their reactions to the psychological abuse may have even left you questioning if your loved one might actually be losing their grip on life or might be "crazy." For some reason, toxic people love to accuse their victims of being crazy. I hear it again and again. Not sure why that particular word but it is a favorite go-to for narcissists, sociopaths, and psychopaths.

I hope to shed some light on why your loved one is or has been struggling with finding stability post-breakup with a toxic person. Let's start with the basics of why this breakup is not like any other relationship your loved one has been in previously, or maybe even you have experienced:

## It Was All A Lie

Your loved one met someone who they had fully and truly fallen in love with and wanted to spend the rest of their life loving. Your loved one was authentic in his or her feelings towards the other person. However, your loved one met a con-artist. The other person only pretended to have feelings for your loved one and strategically set up the entire "relationship" in order to meet her or his own abusive needs.

Toxic people derive great entertainment out of taking a healthy and happy person (your loved one) and completely ruining their life. Hard to imagine, right? As a therapist, I can tell you it is 100% true. Your loved one may have tried to share this information with you, but it was hard for you to believe. You may have even liked the toxic person. Guess what? You were scammed too. Luring in the family and friends is all part of the staged affection the toxic person exhibited. It is done to gain your trust that they are a good honest person. How does this work to their advantage? When your loved one comes and tells you all the nasty and horrible things that happened to them, you question them and their perspective. Maybe you even unknowingly sided with the toxic person against your loved one. Nice move by the abuser. It's all part of the calculated attempt to destroy your loved one and even their relationship with you. Pretty scary if you ask me.

## Not A Normal Break-Up

Telling your loved one to go date again or even better, to go hook up with someone new, isn't going to help the situation at all. Please don't tell your loved one anything close to that advice. The reason that your loved one isn't ready to get out there is because they are a shell of human being right now. Their grief is so complex during the stages of a breakup and recovery that a survivor has no idea which way is the ocean floor and which way is the surface. They are literally drowning in their emotions. Why? Is it because they are weak and need to just get a grip on life? No. Their entire personhood was systematically stripped down and replaced with abuse. The exact traits that your loved one exhibited—that the toxic person initially found appealing—then became the target for destruction.

Your loved one's self-worth and identity have been scrambled by a master manipulator. For example, if your computer got a virus, would you just expect the computer to keep functioning like normal? Why can't the thing just work like it did before?! No you wouldn't. You would realize that your computer had been infected by malware that took over its operating system. This is what has happened to your loved one. They have been poisoned by the exact individual who they thought was their special person in the world. Their rock, their go-to person, their happily-ever-after. It is going to take time for your loved one to deprogram from the abuse; like when someone leaves a cult. Their entire way of seeing themselves and the world around them must be torn down and correctly rebuilt. Just getting out there and dating is not going to help your loved one at all. It actually can stunt their recovery in many ways.

### It Takes As Long As It Takes

I know you want your old loved one back; the one you remember pre-toxic relationship. I know you can see glimmers of him or her at times and then get your hopes up that this nightmare is finally behind you all. In reality, many survivors of psychological abuse develop Post-Traumatic Stress Disorder (PTSD). There are triggers that bring on intense anxiety. Certain times of the year will be harder than others for your loved one. This is normal. Sad, but normal. Why does the abuse cause trauma and a long recovery? Your loved one experienced systematic and repeated covert psychological abuse. The toxic person set out to destroy your loved one. No matter how nice she or he presented to you, listen to what your loved one tells you about the true character of this person. Really listen.

Educate yourself on terms like Gaslighting, Smear Campaigns, Triangulation, Flying Monkeys, Idealize/Devalue/Discard Stage, and Love Bombing. Do yourself and your loved one a huge favor and read the book "Psychopath Free" by Jackson MacKenzie. It is from a survivor's perspective and really truly excellent. Your loved one may ask you to not only read this letter addressed to you, but to read the whole book. Please show your support for your loved one by putting in the time and effort to learn what you can about their life experience.

Above all, believe your loved one when they confide in you that they were abused. Forgive yourself for not noticing the abuse. Come together with your loved one to move forward. The toxic person wanted to destroy your loved one and all of her or his relationships. Please do not let that plan succeed. I wish you all the best as you support your loved one in their recovery. I truly believe better days are ahead for you both.

# ABOUT THE AUTHOR

**Shannon Thomas, LCSW** is a licensed clinical social worker supervisor, and the owner/lead therapist of Southlake Christian Counseling (SCC) in Southlake, Texas.

SCC received the voter award of *Best of 2016: Living Magazine* for "Best Counseling Practice" in the Northeast Tarrant County region of the Dallas-Fort Worth Metroplex.

Ms. Thomas serves as a Field Instructor and Advisory Committee member for the Texas Christian University (TCU) Department of Social Work. She enjoys mentoring the next generation of social workers and therapists.

Her passion is helping people overcome life challenges and seeing her clients living to their fullest potential. Ms. Thomas' life story involves experiencing personal restoration in several areas of her life. She approaches her counseling work from the lens of a licensed therapist and as a fellow survivor of psychological abuse.

Ms. Thomas believes that everyone has a story to tell. You can read more about her story at www.shannonthomas.com.

*Contact Information:*

**Book Website:** www.HealingfromHiddenAbuse.com
Contact Email: Shannon@HealingfromHiddenAbuse.com

**Writer & Speaker Website**: www.ShannonThomas.com

**Business Website:** www.SouthlakeCounseling.org

**Social Media Contact Information:**
Facebook: https://www.facebook.com/SouthlakeChristianCounseling/
Twitter: @SouthlakeLCSW
Instagram: @shannonthomas
Pinterest: @ShannonThomasTX or SCC/Shannon Thomas (Board)

# RESOURCE GUIDE

I have chosen to share these resources with you because they are the exact same ones that I go to on a regular basis. There are numerous books, blogs, and social media accounts out there and many are excellent. What speaks to one person might not be useful to another. Please use this section as a starting point for finding resources that work within your own framework of recovery.

## BOOKS

Shahida Arabi
*Becoming the Narcissist's Nightmare: How to Devalue and Discard the Narcissist While Supplying Yourself*

Dr. Les Carter
*Enough about You, Let's Talk about Me*
*When Pleasing You, Is Killing Me*

Dr. Susan Forward
*Toxic Parents*
*Toxic In-Laws*
*Emotional Blackmail*

Jackson MacKenzie
*Psychopath Free*

Leslie Vernick
*The Emotionally Destructive Marriage*
*The Emotionally Destructive Relationship*

## WEBSITES

Healing from Complex Trauma and PTSD
www.healingfromcomplextraumaandptsd.com

Love Fraud
www.lovefraud.com

Psychopath Free
www.psychopathfree.com

The Smart Girl's Guide to Self-Care
www.selfcarehaven.wordpress.com

## SOCIAL MEDIA

**Instagram**
@Narcissist.sociopath.awarenes2
@selfcarewarrior

**Facebook**
Healing from Complex Trauma and PTSD/CPTSD
International Supporters of Reeva Steenkamp –
    Exposing Narcissistic Abuse
Luke 17:3 Ministries
My Waffles are Cold – A Man's Guide to Abusive Women
Narcissistic and Emotional Abuse

Narcissistic Victim Syndrome – Hope for Victims
    and Survivors
Psychopath Free
Recovering from a Relationship with a Narcissist
    – The Original
The Smart Girl's Guide to Self-Care

**Twitter**
Healing Complex PTSD - @HealingCPTSD
Narcopath Awareness - @narcopathaware
Narcissistic and Emotional Abuse - @NAEAinfo
Psychopath Free - @PscyhopathFree
Shahida Arabi - @selfcarehaven

PERSONAL REFLECTIONS JOURNAL

## Introduction: Journal

Welcome to the personal reflections journal. In writing this material, I am going to assume that you have already read the main book or are in the process of reading it. During our time together in the journal, we will be going deeper into the concepts that are discussed in the book. As a writer, I could have just completed the book, but as a therapist, I believe this section is where you will be able to personalize the six stages of recovery. Being able to take the concepts from *Healing from Hidden Abuse* and bring them to life in your own experience is where true recovery starts. You will be able to do this journaling in the privacy of your own company, with family or friends, or find a local group of survivors who are also navigating through the book. To either be a book study host or participant, please visit www.healingfromhiddenabuse.com. There are groups listed of people who are coming together to support one another in a space that is free from judgment and rich in understanding. No one can comprehend the devastation of hidden psychological abuse quite like another survivor. The idea of survivors walking out of the shadows and into a safe community is precisely why I have estab-

*The idea of survivors walking out of the shadows and into a safe community is precisely why I have established the Find a Book Study option on the* Healing from Hidden Abuse *website.*

lished the Find a Book Study option on the *Healing from Hidden Abuse* website.

The book groups are not intended as a substitute for in-person therapy. Most study groups will be hosted by fellow survivors. The get-togethers should not become informal therapy unless a licensed counselor is the book study host. The book groups should be a place where survivors can show up, find mutual support, healthy boundaries among group members, and the ability for all survivors to be welcomed no matter where they are in their recovery. The structure of the book study group will be determined by the individuals who step up to host. Some groups will be men only, women only, mixed groups, groups for those who have gone No Contact, survivors who have implemented Detached Contact, or any combination of book study members. There might be book study groups dealing specifically with hidden psychological abuse in a romantic relationship, workplace, or religious setting. There are endless ideas of how the book could be used for local peer facilitated support. My role is merely to provide an online option of survivors being introduced to one another in their local area.

From there, it is up to the host and book study members to create a group that meets their unique needs.

Regardless of whether you are going to journal on your own—or in a book study—I encourage you to be alert to how you are feeling during the process. Some of what we will be talking about could be triggering, and difficult memories might emerge. Please take your time. Be mindful of your emotional and physical well-being. There is no rush to finish the book or journal. Slow down and breathe. When needed, put the materials away, and come back to them another day. It is also wonderful to take small snippets of the book each day. This allows you to meditate on the concept you read for that specific day. Many people choose to read a page, or group of questions, and let that be enough. You may want to go through the material quickly, and that is great too. The bottom line is that your recovery journey is your own. You get to decide the best approach for your healing. With that in mind, if you visit a local book study group and it doesn't have the right vibe or attitude, visit other groups until you find one that works best for you. Perhaps you will enjoy this journal as an individual journey and that is a wonderful option as well. Recovery from psychological abuse is an intensely individual experience and it cannot be rushed. Since there are different levels of severity to trauma, there will also be a variance in the length of time survivors feel ready to move forward into the next stage of recovery.

I want to pause here and say that I am terribly sorry that you need to heal at all. Hidden psychological abuse is cryptic, silent, and very misunderstood. As a survivor, you know all this to be true. Trust me when I say that once you have finished the six stages of recovery, you will know more about abuse from personality disordered people than most practicing therapists. It is personally impactful when you can put specific names of people and life situations to the material covered in *Healing from Hidden Abuse*. This journal section will be a series of questions and short moments of discussion. In all, my hope is that through the practice of journaling—and maybe sharing the process within a book study group—that you will glean deeper wisdom from your individual story.

## *Who* is a Psychological Abuser?

Who are these people? A narcissist, sociopath, or psychopath could be your mom, dad, brother, sister, grandparent, aunt, uncle, cousin, boyfriend, girlfriend, husband, wife, adult child, friend, in-laws, co-worker, boss, pastor, mentor, or any other title that exists in human relationships. As you can see, their toxicity can impact many people. Their circle of influence (and therefore destruction) is sadly widespread.

I will intermittently use the terms "toxic person" or "toxic people." I am referring to those individuals who fit the criteria for Narcissistic Personality Disorder (aka the narcissist) and Anti-Social Personality Disorder (aka the sociopath or psychopath). I understand that you may not know for sure if the abuser would fit the diagnosis criteria, and that is perfectly okay.

*In your own words, please describe the different characteristics of a narcissist, sociopath, and psychopath.*

*Narcissist:* _____

_____

_____

Sociopath: _____

_____

_____

_____

_____

Psychopath: _____

_____

_____

_____

_____

People often ask what the clinical differences are between a narcissist, sociopath, and psychopath. I will use these fictional examples to highlight the subtle differences:

**A Narcissist** will run you over and scold you for being in their way. They will endlessly complain about how you damaged their car.

**A Sociopath** will run you over, scold you for being in their way, and have a smirk because secretly they get entertainment out of the chaos they've created.

**A Psychopath** will go to great lengths and take calculated steps to ensure they run you over, laugh while doing it, and back up to make sure the most damage is done.

Lovely people, right? That is precisely why you are doing the hard work to use Detached Contact or No Contact with these toxic individuals. If those terms are new to you, no need to worry. You will learn all about them in our time together.

*Given the above example of the fictional car, how does your definition of a narcissist, sociopath, and psychopath change, or stay the same from what you initially wrote?*

## Gender and Abuse

The stereotype is that only men are narcissists, sociopaths, and psychopaths. That is completely incorrect. There are many women who are the cause of a toxic relationship, family, workplace, or church setting.

*Please share how female and male psychological abusers might be alike and different based on gender:*

*Common Qualities:* _____

_____

_____

_____

_____

*Different Qualities:* _____

_____

_____

_____

_____

*Please share a brief summary of the psychological abuse you experienced from one or both genders:*

*Female:* _____

_____

_____

_____

*Male:* _____

_____

_____

_____

*If you experienced abuse from both genders, how did the abuse differ as it related to gender?* _____

_____

---

---

---

*How has your recovery process differed depending on the gender of the abuser?* _____

---

---

---

---

If a victim has a hard time proving physical violence, it is even harder to get people to take psychological abuse seriously. Survivors who try to get help to protect themselves and their children are often seen as "hysterical, crazy, and unstable." This is because the covert nature of hidden abuse is very difficult to put into words. Without the correct language, survivors often sound obsessed. Those of us in the recovery community know that is not the issue at all. The general public still has much to learn about hidden psychological abuse.

*In a short description, please write what you have said to others to describe the abuse you have experienced.* ___

---

---

---

_____

_____

*How well has your description been received by your family, friends, co-workers, or church leadership?* _____

_____

_____

_____

_____

*In your opinion, why is psychological abuse so hard to describe to someone who has not experienced it?* _____

_____

_____

_____

_____

### *What* is a Psychological Abuser?

Narcissists, sociopaths, and psychopaths walk among us. It's true. As a therapist, I can diagnosis adults as Narcissistic Personality Disordered (NPD) or Anti-Social Personality Disordered (ASPD). We do not typically diagnose personality disorders before the individual has reached adulthood. The thinking is that personalities are still forming throughout the teenage years. Some people do show characteristics of NPD or ASPD early on in life, and those kids or teens are often given other diagnoses that are not personality related.

*Did you ever attempt counseling or some form of mediation with your abuser? If yes, what was that experience like for you? If you have not done so, what challenges do you think there would be in attempting to address issues with a third person present?* _____

_____

_____

_____

_____

_____

*Do you believe everyone is a "little narcissistic." If yes, please share why you believe this to be true. If no, please share why you do not see narcissism in everyone.* _____

_____

_____

_____

_____

_____

*Do you believe in the concept of "healthy narcissism?" If yes, please share your definition of healthy narcissism.*

*If no, please share why you do not believe there are forms of healthy narcissism.* _____

_____

_____

_____

_____

I have some fairly strong beliefs against the idea that everyone is a little narcissistic or that there can be healthy forms of narcissism. Narcissistic Personality Disorder (NPD) is a distortion of a normally formed sense of self. The diagnosis reflects a personality that did not develop correctly from childhood and beyond. In adulthood, these individuals choose to remain abusive. It is beyond my reasoning that any part of narcissism, sociopathy or psychopathy can be healthy. It is like saying that there are healthy cancer cells.

There are certain criteria that must be met for the diagnosis of NPD and ASPD. Either the person meets the specific guidelines or they do not. There is no such thing as a little narcissism from a clinical perspective. Either someone fits the diagnosis or another one must be selected in which they do meet the criteria. We get the idea of "healthy narcissism" from the diagnostic tool Narcissistic Personality Inventory (NPI). It is a deeply flawed resource because it assesses people who are suspected of having perception distortions (the toxic person). They are asked to take a self-administered questionnaire, where it is easy to see which answer will give a grandiose impression. Most suspected personality disordered people are keen enough to know how to read a room and manipulate people. They are aware of how to keep from looking "bad" when it serves their interests.

Some researchers and mental health professionals look at a low score on the NPI and conclude that the individuals taking the test have a "little narcissism." Seriously, that is where the term comes from and it is beyond ridiculous to me. Just because someone shows significant levels of self-esteem, self-reliance, and maybe even a bit of bravado, does not indicate that they are void of empathy and enjoy harming others for entertainment. Those are character traits of someone with Narcissistic Personality Disorder or Anti-Social Personality Disorder.

It is perfectly okay if you still believe in the idea of healthy narcissism or that everyone is a little narcissistic. We don't have to see eye to eye on every concept because respect for differences is something narcissists, sociopaths, and psychopaths cannot comprehend. Advocates and survivors in the psychological abuse community will not mirror anything that a psychological abuser would embody. Out of respect, we do not force our viewpoints on others.

### *Where* do psychological abusers do their harm?

Abuse can happen from one individual to another (example: parent-child, a romantic relationship, workplace, or friendship) or within a group (example: family members, workplace, groups of people, or religious organization).

*Did your abuse take place in an:*
*Individual relationship—Within a group—Both?*
*(Please circle which one applies to you)*

*Share about a relationship with an individual that was or is psychologically abusive. If you do not have one, please share what you think would be most hurtful about abuse between one individual to another.* _____

_____

_____

_____

_____

_____

*Share about a relationship with a group that was or is psychologically abusive. If you have not experienced one, please share why abuse from a group of people would be challenging for a survivor.* _____

_____

_____

_____

_____

_____

## Individual Abusers

### *Toxic Love Interest or Spouse:*

There are many different ways that a romantic partner can perpetrate hidden psychological abuse. I have witnessed some of the most hateful and evil abuse occur within what was intended to be a safe relationship.

*If the abuse is within a romantic relationship, share what has been the number one most difficult part of psychological abuse by a love interest or spouse. If your abuse did not take place with a romantic interest, share what you perceive to be one of the hardest components of psychological abuse in a romantic relationship.* _____

_____

_____

_____

_____

_____

*If the abuse took place in a romantic relationship, what is one memory that was a very low point in the relationship?* _____

_____

_____

_____

_____

*At what moment did you know you were dealing with a toxic person while in a romantic relationship? What were the specific circumstances?* _____

_____

_____

_____

_____

*In hindsight, do you now wish you had ended the romantic relationship at that time? If no, why?* _____

_____

_____

_____

_____

*If yes, what kept you from doing so at the time? What fears or life hindrances were there for you to end the re-*

*lationship?* _____

_____

_____

_____

_____

*If you did not end the relationship when you wish you had, what steps have you taken to forgive yourself for staying longer?* _____

_____

_____

_____

_____

## The Toxic Friend

Friendships are at the core of our regular support system. They are what enriches our lives in numerous ways. Our friends are the family members that we get to choose. Since friends have such personal access to us and our private thoughts, choosing wisely is critically important. We all have had a friendship where we wondered why we let that particular person close to us.

*If you have had a toxic friendship, please give a few details about the who, what, where, when, how, and why of that friendship. If you have had more than one toxic friend, pick the one that comes to mind right now. If your abuse did not take place within a friendship, share what you perceive to be one of the hardest components of psychological abuse in a peer relationship.* _____

_____

_____

_____

_____

*If you are still in contact with the toxic friend, what keeps you in that relationship?* _____

_____

_____

_____

_____

*If you have No Contact, what was the point in which the friendship ended?* _____

_____

_____

_____

_____

## Group of Abusers

*The Toxic Family*

The hateful and stinging words of a psychologically abusive parent can linger in the mind of an adult child long after the adult has left home. This is because narcissists, sociopaths, or psychopaths make terrible parents. They lack the basic empathy and selfless nature that loving parenting requires. They have no problem meeting their own needs first before their children's needs. They feel completely justified in their actions. Abusers create valid resentments and later in life, wonder why they have no authentic relationship with their adult children. Chronic selfishness and parenting do not go together.

*If you are a survivor of psychological abuse from your family of origin, please provide one example of hidden abuse from the family. If you are not a survivor of family abuse, please share one reason why you think this form of abuse might take longer for recovery compared to another type of abusive environment.* _____

_____

_____

_____

_____

There is a clinical term called "pseudomutuality" and it applies to many toxic families. The term describes those families that appear to have a high level of connection and agreement, but in fact, they have very dysfunctional and harmful relationships behind the public image. The façade to the world is a close knit family, but the reality is something very different and highly destructive.

*In your own words, please describe "pseudomutality" as it relates to psychologically abusive family relationships that you have experienced. If you have not had an abusive family relationship, please share how you see pseudomutality in another toxic environment.* _____

_____

_____

_____

_____

_____

*Describe a time when you were caught in the "Venus fly-trap" of a toxic family. What was used to lure you into the trap? If you have not experienced abuse within a toxic family, what other environments have you experienced the use of the "Venus fly-trap" method?* _____

_____

_____

_____

_____

_____

*Once you were lured into the trap, how and when did the friendliness of the environment shift?* _____

_____

_____

_____

_____

_____

Belonging is at the core of our human experience. We are hard wired to need and want to be included. Everyone desires to know that we have people and our people have us. It is this exact human necessity that abusers exploit for their own gain.

*What are a few specific ways that your abuser(s) made you feel like you did not belong?* _____

_____

_____

_____

_____

_____

*What was your emotional response following this mistreatment?* _____

_____

_____

_____

_____

### The Toxic Church: Its Leadership and Members

Why is it that a lot of people are cautious about things that have to do with Christianity? I think it's because there are far too many pastors and ministry leaders out there running amok in the name of God. They are doing a lot of harm in the process—damaging people who are trying to find God in the blur of modern life. Let me pause here and be clear that I am not saying all pastors or ministry leaders are awful. I am saying some, if not many, are miserable examples of the wonderful character qualities of love, patience, kindness, and hope. I have been a part of churches and ministries for over 20 years. I have seen the best and the worst Christianity has to offer.

*Did you experience abuse within a religious setting? If so, please share an overview of what occurred. If you have not been spiritually abused, share why you believe this form of abuse would be complex for recovery.* _____

_____

_____

_____

_____

_____

*What are three specific Scriptures or Biblical teachings that were used against you by the psychological abuser(s)?*

_____

_____

_____

_____

_____

*Pick one of the above Scriptures or Biblical teachings and share how the abuser distorted its meaning to suit his or her agenda of abuse.* _____

_____

_____

_____

_____

*In your own words, what do you believe is the real meaning of the above Scripture or teaching that you picked?* _____

_____

_____

_____

_____

Many people still believe that all narcissists, sociopaths, and psychopaths are overtly grandiose and obvious in their toxic behaviors. After spending decades immersed in church culture, I can assure you that not all psychological abusers are outwardly grandiose. In a religious setting, outward appearance of humility is highly regarded, and grandiosity would be frowned upon. Therefore, toxic people hiding in church communities will take on the mannerisms and communication patterns of those around them. These psychological abusers do not fit the standard image or teaching of how to spot a personality disordered person. We must become educated as to the various personas that toxic people can manifest in order to hide their abusive behaviors.

*Why do you think it is easy for narcissists, sociopaths, and psychopaths to hide in church communities (whether on staff or as a congregation member)?* _____

_____

_____

_____

_____

*What will need to change about modern church culture for psychological abusers to be identified quicker and firm boundaries set in order to keep congregation members safe from harm?* _____

_____

_____

_____

_____

_____

*Do you believe religious women experience a higher level of hidden psychological abuse than religious men? Please share your reasoning to your answer.* _____

_____

_____

_____

_____

*Since narcissists, sociopaths, and psychopaths submit their will to no one, do you believe it is possible for them to have an authentic relationship with God? How does this impact a toxic person's ability to seek God's guidance and receive positive influences in their lives?* _____

_____

_____

_____

_____

### The Toxic Workplace

Narcissists, sociopaths, and psychopaths have to earn a living. Guess where they end up? As employees, co-workers, managers, or senior level executives. Toxic people in the workplace often use very covert methods of undermining a survivor's success. This can look like chronically not giving the survivor all the information needed to complete an assignment, and then embarrassing them when the task is not as it should be. Sometimes the abuse is not covert, but very overt and aggressive. Again, there are many ways that psychological abusers can manifest their dysfunctions. Survivors have shared that in the workplace they have been aggressively yelled at, publicly mocked, and even physically touched in a manner meant as an act of dominance.

_Did you experience abuse within a workplace? If so, please share an overview of what occurred. If you have not been psychologically abused at work, share why you believe this form of abuse would be complex for setting boundaries._ _____

_____

_____

_____

*Do other people know of the abuse you are, or were, experiencing? If so, what did they do to help you, or did they look the other way? If no one knows, what stops you from telling anyone?* _____

_____

_____

_____

_____

*What coping skills help, or helped, you deal with psychological abuse in the workplace?* _____

_____

_____

_____

_____

## *When* do psychological abusers harm others?

Abusers like to target people who have something they do not or cannot possess themselves. Narcissists, sociopaths, and psychopaths are notorious for picking targets that initially boost their egos. It could be the target's appearance, age, intellect, reputation, religious convictions, career success, family, friends, or something else. Once the target is hooked, the toxic person then sets out to tear down the exact qualities that attracted her or him to the survivor in the first place. It is a source of power and entertainment for a toxic person to destroy an originally healthy and happy person. This point is often missed by survivors because in the middle of the abuse, they see themselves as broken. Since the abuser says such hateful things, the survivor assumes they were targeted because they are "weak." That is the exact opposite of the truth. Targets who hold no value to abusers won't even be bothered with, and a bigger "prize" would have originally been found. Psychological abusers like people who make them look or feel good. Much like leeches, they attach themselves to people who give them sustenance of some sort. Once they have had their fill, the abuser will begin the process of destroying the qualities of the survivor that produce jealous feelings in the abuser. Since toxic people cannot possess certain positive attributes, they do not want the survivor to have them either.

*What three qualities do you have, or had, that were attractive to the narcissist, sociopath, or psychopath?* ___

_____

_____

_____

_____

*Share the specific details of when the psychological abuser first started tearing down your self-esteem.* _____

_____

_____

_____

_____

_____

*What was your response to the shift in the relation-ship?* _____

_____

_____

_____

*Did you ever notice jealousy about your success, physical appearance, financial stability, or any other positive aspect of your life? If so, what was the focus of their jealousy?* _____

_____

_____

_____

*What happened that made you realize they were jealous of you?* _____

_____

_____

_____

_____

_____

### *How* do psychological abusers harm others?

Toxic people are great actors. They will utilize which-ever props are available to maintain control in the re-lationship. For example, some psychological abusers will use tears when it serves to make them look like the victim. They may also use outward expressions of emo-tions when needing to look like they have changed, but are actually attempting to manipulate the survivor back into the toxic games. Manipulative people use a wide range of fake emotions to try and control those around them. In addition to tears, they may use guilt in an effort to make a survivor feel badly for setting boundaries. A toxic person can utilize anger to intimidate people into being compliant. They may try to appear overly happy in an effort to make a survivor feel discarded and for-gotten. The important point to remember is that most outwardly expressed emotions of psychological abusers are for a distinct purpose; that is usually to harm others in some way. Their actions cannot be trusted nor can they be taken at face value. Psychological abusers have perfected the use of their acting skills for a reason.

Psychological abuse is not a one-and-done type

of abuse. I often relate the process that survivors go through as "collecting pebbles." One pebble represents a single, negative encounter with a psychological abuser.

*Did your abuser ever use tears as a form of manipulation? If no, what was their "go-to" emotion in order to get what they wanted?* _____

_____

_____

_____

_____

*In hindsight, what was the very first red-flag the abuser showed?* _____

_____

_____

_____

_____

*Describe some of the "pebbles" that the psychological abuser showed.* _____

_____

_____

_____

_____

_____

### *Why* do Psychological Abusers Harm Others?

I do a lot of reading, listening to podcasts, and radio shows on the topic of narcissism, sociopathy, psychopathy, and the recovery from this type of abuse. I can tell you there are different camps of people out there who propose a wide range of beliefs about the development of personality disorders. Some argue that there is a spectrum of what we should expect as normal human character flaws. Narcissism seems to be the gray area where most discord bubbles up. Common teachings on sociopaths and psychopaths center on their intense lack of empathy. Hollywood has even attempted to paint a picture of how people with personality disorders behave. Some of these characters are true reflections of the disorders, and some are merely Hollywood attempts at making an exciting movie or television show.

*Do you believe people with personality disorders have a "mental illness?"* _____

_____

*In your own words, how are personality disorders created, or do you believe people are born narcissists, sociopaths, and psychopaths?* _____

_____

_____

_____

_____

_____

*In your opinion, how does the role of attachment influence personality disorders?* _____

_____

_____

_____

_____

*Do you believe narcissists, sociopaths, and psychopaths know they are abusive to other people?* _____

_____

_____

_____

_____

*Are narcissists, sociopaths, and psychopaths capable of making permanent positive changes in their behaviors?*

_____

_____

_____

_____

_____

## Common Character Traits of Survivors

We have spent some time looking at who, what, where, when, how, and why psychological abuse occurs. I want to pause and talk briefly about what I have noticed in the survivors of this type of abuse. Targets of hidden abuse seem to have a few important and common character qualities. Some are positive, and some definitely need to be managed.

_Do you consider yourself a highly adaptive (flexible) person?_ _____

_____

_____

_Do you believe your personal "brokenness" attracted the psychological abuser to you? If so, what was wounded within you that you felt was used against you?_ _____

_____

_____

_____

_____

_____

*What is your definition of codependency?* _____

_____

_____

_____

_____

_____

*Do you believe you are or have ever been codependent? If so, how has that impacted your recovery from psychological abuse?* _____

_____

_____

_____

_____

*What is your definition of an Empath?* _____

_____

_____

_____

_____

_____

*Do you identify as being a highly empathetic person?*
*If so, how has your empathy been used against you by the*
*psychological abuser?* _____

_____

_____

_____

_____

_____

Toxic environments bring out poor behaviors in even the most patient of individuals. Survivors of psychological abuse find themselves behaving in ways that don't fit their normal personality. This shift can serve as a red flag that the environment is unhealthy. The change in survivors can sadly also fuel any toxic gossip being spread by abusive individuals or groups of people.

*What are three moments that you wish you could do*
*over because of your behavior with the abuser(s)?* _____

_____

_____

_____

_____

_____

*How have you been able to forgive yourself for actions that did not fit your view of yourself?* _____

_____

_____

_____

_____

_____

*What actions or thoughts currently help, or helped you, to keep the "spotlight" on the psychological abuser and not move it to yourself by your behaviors?* _____

_____

_____

_____

_____

_____

## Stage One: Despair (Journal)

When survivors first begin counseling for psychological abuse recovery, many don't even know they have been abused. They do know life has become unmanageable, and they are looking for answers. Some don't yet understand the full depth of what has been done to them by the abuser(s). At the beginning of counseling, survivors are (more times than not) in emotional chaos, anxious, depressed, or suicidal. Sometimes all of the above and more. The very first place we start is their safety to not harm themselves. Once that has been established, we begin the work of identifying the despair the survivor feels. The first stage of recovery can be a scary season in life. Luckily, several more stages follow, and hope begins to shine through.

*During the abuse, did you ever feel like harming yourself? (If you now feel that you want to harm yourself, please immediately call 911, or go to your nearest emergency room.) If you answered yes to the above question, what stopped you from previously causing harm to yourself?* _____

_____

_____

_____

_____

_____

*While in the Despair stage, what are three coping skills or activities that help, or helped, you get through difficult moments?* _____

_____

_____

_____

_____

_____

*Do you, or have you, ever blamed yourself for the psychological abuse?* _____

_____

_____

_____

_____

*What was your "I can't do this anymore" moment? If you have not reached that point in the relationship yet, what would have to occur for you to feel ready to make significant changes in the relationship with the psychological abuser?* _____

_____

_____

_____

_____

## Stage Two: Education (Journal)

Psychological abuse is exceptionally insidious and therefore misunderstood. That is precisely part of the abuser(s) tactic to keep the abuse hidden and remain firmly in control. A victim cannot begin recovery if they can't describe what has been done to them. Learning the common methods employed by psychological abusers is *Stage Two*. Survivors new to recovery should know what the following terms mean in relationship to psychological abuse:

- Gaslighting
- Smear Campaign
- Flying Monkeys
- Narcissistic Offense
- Intermittent Reinforcement
- Idealize, Devalue, and Discard Phases

There are other terms, but for *Stage Two*, this list is a great starting point for those seeking recovery.

*In your own words, please describe **Gaslighting**.* ____

_____

_____

_____

_____

*Give a specific example of when you experienced Gas-lighting by a psychological abuser.* _____

_____

_____

_____

_____

*What makes Gaslighting so dangerous to survivors?*

_____

_____

_____

_____

*In your own words, please describe **Smear Campaign**.*

_____

_____

_____

_____

*Give a specific example of when you experienced a Smear Campaign by a psychological abuser.* _____

_____

_____

_____

_____

*Why is being the target of a Smear Campaign emotionally painful?* _____

_____

_____

_____

*In your own words, please describe **Flying Monkeys**.*

_____

_____

_____

_____

*Give a specific example of when you experienced Flying Monkeys in the context of a relationship with a psychological abuser.* _____

_____

_____

_____

_____

*What is the most frustrating aspect of dealing with Flying Monkeys?* _____

_____

_____

_____

_____

*In your own words, please describe **Narcissistic Offense** (aka Toxic Person Offense).* _____

_____

_____

_____

_____

*Give a specific example of when you experienced Narcissistic Offense by a psychological abuser.* _____

_____

_____

_____

_____

*Why do toxic people become easily offended?* _____

_____

_____

_____

_____

*In your own words, please describe* **Intermittent Rein-forcement.** _____

_____

_____

_____

_____

*Give a specific example of when you experienced Intermittent Reinforcement by a psychological abuser.* ____

_____

_____

_____

_____

*What makes the yo-yo experience of Intermittent Reinforcement so painful?* _____

_____

_____

_____

*In your own words, please describe the **Idealize Phase**.*

_____

_____

_____

_____

*Give a specific example of when you experienced the Idealize Phase by a psychological abuser.* _____

_____

_____

_____

_____

*What do you miss most about the Idealize Phase?* ___

_____

_____

_____

_____

*In your own words, please describe the **Devalue Phase**.* _____

_____

_____

*Give a specific example of when you experienced the Devalue Phase by a psychological abuser.* _____

_____

_____

_____

_____

*Do you remember the exact moment, or season, when the Devalue Phase showed up in your relationship?* \_\_\_\_\_

_____

_____

_____

_____

*In your own words, please describe the **Discard Phase.***

_____

_____

_____

_____

*Give a specific example of when you experienced the Discard Phase by a psychological abuser.* _____

_____

_____

_____

_____

How did the discard take place? Were you forced to do it or did the abuser do the discard? If you have Detached Contact, what was the moment when you knew something had to change in the relationship? _____

_____

_____

_____

_____

Are there other terms within the psychological abuse recovery community that have helped you grow in your understanding of hidden abuse? _____

_____

_____

_____

_____

## Stage Three: Awakening (Journal)

When survivors have identified their *Despair* from having been psychologically abused (Stage One), and then *Educated* themselves on the specific ways abusers harm others (Stage Two), an *Awakening* happens for the survivor (Stage Three). This is the point in recovery when many aha moments happen. Survivors can describe what they experienced, have learned new terminology, and in doing so, no longer feel isolated in the abuse. At this stage, a survivor may start to feel empowered in their recovery journey. However, there are good days and bad days. It is common for survivors to swing back to *Despair* and then forward to *Awakening* again. This is normal and part of the process of deprogramming and healing from the psychological abuse.

*Describe your key aha moment in recovery.* _____

_____

_____

_____

_____

*Survivors often come to a place of making statements like, "How dare they treat me like this?" What is, or was, one sentence that you find yourself repeating during the Awakening stage?* _____

_____

_____

_____

*Is Stage Three: Awakening hopeful, sad, or both?* _____

_____

_____

_____

*Have you been able to connect with other survivors or do you feel isolated in your experience of being a survivor of psychological abuse?* _____

_____

_____

_____

_____

## Stage Four: Boundaries (Journal)

After a survivor of psychological abuse has identified their *Despair* (Stage One), *Educated* themselves on the specifics of psychological abuse (Stage Two), and had an *Awakening* that recovery is possible (Stage Three), the next stage is implementing *Boundaries*. This is the time when survivors choose to implement Detached Contact or No Contact. The important part of this stage is that a survivor is able to gain enough emotional distance to detox from the trauma bonding and start looking forward to their life of recovery. Boundaries are individually driven and must be done in a way that will be followed through on by the survivor. At times, survivors waiver on setting limits with their abuser(s). To set healthy limits may mean the end of the relationship. It is not uncommon for some survivors to get stuck at this stage.

*Are you currently in counseling or would you be willing to try to find a counselor who "gets it?" If no, please share why.* _____

_____

_____

_Are you utilizing Detached Contact, No Contact, or a combination of both if there is more than one abuser?_ __

_____

_____

_____

_____

_What is one boundary that is, or was, the hardest to set and maintain? What has made it difficult?_ _____

_____

_____

_____

_____

_When you think, or had thoughts, about setting boundaries with the psychological abuser, what are three inner thoughts that hinder(ed) you?_ _____

_____

_____

_____

_____

*Examples:*
*I will be alone.*
*This job is the only path to reach my career goals.*
*This church is the only one God is really using in a dynamic way to do His will.*
*Your family will always be there, but friends come and go.*

*What did you find interesting when you completed the Balanced Life journaling exercise? _____*

_____

_____

_____

_____

*Have you ever struggled with feeling like you were being too sensitive or overreacting when thinking about setting boundaries? _____*

_____

_____

_____

_____

Detached Contact is exactly as it sounds, and it involves more than just limiting time. It is the posturing of the survivor's heart. There are interactions still between the abuser and the survivor, but the tone is radically different than before the abuse was uncovered and understood by the survivor. Detached Contact is about the emotional state of the survivor.

*In your own words, please describe* **Detached Contact.** _____

_____

_____

_____

*When would Detached Contact be the best option or the only option for a survivor?* _____

_____

_____

_____

*What do you believe is the biggest challenge in maintaining Detached Contact with a psychological abuser?*

_____

_____

_____

_____

*Do you believe it is possible for a survivor to live a life of true recovery and still have some contact with a toxic person?* _____

_____

_____

_____

Now we are at the point where cutting ties with psychological abusers is the best option for some survivors' situations. While this path has its own set of challenges, once the removal of toxicity has occurred and the dust has settled, having No Contact is the most concrete way of moving forward and away from abuse.

*In your own words, please describe going* **No Contact** *with a psychological abuser.* _____

_____

_____

_____

_____

*When would No Contact be the best option or the only option for a survivor?* _____

_____

_____

_____

_____

*What do you believe is the biggest challenge in maintaining No Contact with a psychological abuser?* _____

_____

_____

_____

_____

*What are three key things to remember when in No Contact with an abuser?* _____

_____

_____

_____

_____

*Which choice do you believe requires the most advanced level of coping skills and recovery knowledge: Detached Contact or No Contact, and why?* _____

_____

_____

_____

_____

## Stage Five: Restoration (Journal)

After a survivor of psychological abuse has identified their *Despair* (Stage One), *Educated* themselves on the specifics of psychological abuse (Stage Two), had an *Awakening* that recovery is possible (Stage Three), and implemented *Boundaries* (Stage Four), the next stage is the *Restoration* of the material items, life event moments, financial stability, physical health, mental health, or any other losses the survivor identifies as having been stolen during the season of abuse. This should be an encouraging stage as survivors start to tangibly see the fruits of their recovery work. Restoration can take longer than survivors expect so patience with the process of recovery is vitally important. Without patience, a survivor can become easily discouraged.

One of the first signs that survivors have reached this stage in recovery is when they feel the desire to spend their free time on activities unrelated to recovery education. Survivors describe entering this stage as having come to a point of saturation regarding all the new knowledge they have found for themselves. Often, people long to pull away from the online forums and other reading materials about narcissism, sociopathy, and psychopathy. This is not a rejection of the people or experiences survivors have enjoyed in order to find healing; it is actually a positive indicator that normalcy is returning. Maybe it is occurring for the first time, as in the case of childhood abuse. Survivors in this stage of recovery feel an attraction to new hobbies and ways to enrich their lives. This longing is wonderful and can serve as a catalyst for fresh adventures.

*How did you know, or will you know, that you have reached Stage Five: Restoration?* _____

_____

_____

_____

_____

*Describe one incident when a holiday, vacation, or other celebration was ruined by the psychological abuser.*

_____

_____

_____

_____

*What is one action you can take to enjoy the next holiday, vacation, or celebration?* _____

_____

_____

_____

*How did the abuser create chaos financially, either through very rigid spending rules or excessive spending?*

_____

_____

_____

_____

*What is one action that you can take in order to heal from financial abuse?* _____

_____

_____

_____

_____

*How has your physical health been impacted by the hidden abuse?* _____

_____

_____

_____

_____

*What is one action you can take to begin healing your physical body?* _____

_____

_____

_____

_____

*How has your emotional well-being been affected by the psychological abuser?* _____

_____

_____

_____

_____

*What is one way you will recognize that your emotional health is returning?* _____

_____

_____

_____

_____

*Name one special item that was destroyed or stolen during the abuse?* _____

_____

_____

_____

_____

*You may not be able to replace the exact item, but what are three actions you can take to help restore what was taken? (Example: if a beloved painting was destroyed, find another piece of artwork that speaks to you and purchase it.)* _____

_____

_____

_____

_____

## Stage Six: Maintenance (Journal)

After a survivor of psychological abuse has identified their *Despair* (Stage One), *Educated* themselves on the specifics of psychological abuse (Stage Two), had an *Awakening* that recovery is possible (Stage Three), implemented *Boundaries* (Stage Four), and experienced *Restoration* of losses during the abuse (Stage Five), the final stage of recovery from psychological abuse is *Maintenance*. During this sixth and last stage, survivors will often willingly loop back to earlier stages and experience deeper levels of healing. The *Maintenance* stage also involves being able to experience healthy relationships going forward and identify toxic people quicker than previously. Maintenance is when a survivor fully lives their life of recovery with the confidence and skills to keep themselves safe from future abuse.

Welcome, friend, to the last stage of recovery! Does that mean you now will never struggle with post-traumatic stress symptoms, never think of the abuser, and will always run through the hills singing songs of jubilance? Of course not. You have made it to a very high mountain top, so please slow down enough to enjoy the view. The air is fresher here and your senses are heightened. This is the point in the journey of healing from psychological abuse that dedicating yourself to living clean becomes the new norm. When you have traveled the journey you have, and fought to find peace, you are less likely to willingly go back to the pits of despair. I saw a quote that said, "When we know how to be happy, we won't tolerate being around someone who makes us unhappy." That is the truth.

*How has reaching Stage Six: Maintenance been different than you expected?* _____

_____

_____

_____

_____

*What has been the hardest part of your recovery journey so far?* _____

_____

_____

_____

_____

*Please share a time when you saw a red-flag in another person and set a quick boundary?* _____

_____

_____

_____

_____

*What has been the best part of your recovery journey so far?* _____

_____

_____

_____

_____

*If you could give a survivor new to recovery one piece of advice, what would it be?* _____

_____

_____

_____

_____

*How will you reward yourself for having reached this huge personal growth milestone?* _____

_____

_____

_____

Access to you is a gift. The ability to call you, text you, e-mail you, see you, come to your home, and basically share space in your life is earned, not easily given. At least it should be. It is yours to parcel out as you choose.

*Please list three people who have earned the right through their own emotional health to have access to you.* _____

_____

_____

_____

*Please list three people who do not have access to you.*

_____

_____

_____

_____

As we conclude our time together, this is a great journaling exercise: Ask yourself the question, "What is a high-quality life for me?" This question is not about what other people think your life should look like or you trying to keep up with anyone else's life. This is a deeply personal and individual question. Often times, people will include living in a way that has a redemptive quality from past experiences.